WHAT IS THE BOOK OF GENESIS?

Kids' Guides to God's Word Series

What Is the Book of Genesis?
What Is the Book of Exodus?
What Is the Book of Leviticus?
What Is the Book of Numbers?
What Is the Book of Deuteronomy?
What Is the Book of Joshua?
What Is the Book of Judges?
What Is the Book of Ruth?
What Is the Book of 1 Samuel?
What Is the Book of 2 Samuel?
What Is the Book of 1 Kings?
What Is the Book of 2 Kings?
What Are the Books of 1–2 Chronicles?
What Are the Books of Ezra & Nehemiah?
What Is the Book of Esther?
What Is the Book of Job?
What Is the Book of Psalms?
What Is the Book of Proverbs?
What Is the Book of Ecclesiastes?
What Are the Books of Song of Songs &
Lamentations?
What Is the Book of Isaiah?
What Is the Book of Jeremiah?
What Is the Book of Ezekiel?
What Is the Book of Daniel?
What Are the Books of Hosea–Micah?
What Are the Books of Nahum–Malachi?

What Is the Gospel of Matthew?
What Is the Gospel of Mark?
What Is the Gospel of Luke?
What Is the Gospel of John?
What Is the Book of Acts?
What Is the Book of Romans?
What Is the Book of 1 Corinthians?
What Is the Book of 2 Corinthians?
What Is the Book of Galatians?
What Is the Book of Ephesians?
What Is the Book of Philippians?
What Are the Books of Colossians
& Philemon?
What Are the Books of 1–2 Thessalonians?
What Are the Books of 1–2 Timothy & Titus?
What Is the Book of Hebrews?
What Is the Book of James?
What Are the Books of 1–2 Peter & Jude?
What Are the Books of 1-3 John?
What Is the Book of Revelation?

What Is the Book of

GENESIS?

Michael Whitworth

ISBN 978-1-971767-04-8

Published by Start2Finish
Bend, Oregon 97702
start2finish.org

Printed in the United States of America

30 29 28 27 26   1 2 3 4 5

For my daughter Audrey—

*May you always trust in the promises,
provision, and goodness of the God of Abraham.
Especially when the story doesn't make sense.*

He is always faithful. He always has been.

Daddy loves you.

CONTENTS

INTRODUCTION

Have you ever started a movie twenty minutes late? Everyone else has been watching from the beginning. They know who the characters are, why the villain is angry, what the hero is trying to do. But you walked in during the middle of a chase scene, and now you're leaning over to someone whispering, "Wait—who's that guy? Why is she running? What's in the briefcase?" That's what it's like to read most of the Bible without reading Genesis first.

Genesis is the beginning of everything. If you skip it, you'll spend the next sixty-five books wondering why things are the way they are. Why is there evil in the world? Why does God care so much about one particular family? Why does blood keep showing up every time someone needs to be forgiven? Why does God make promises and then take so long to keep them? Why does the Bible keep talking about a "seed" and a land and a blessing that's supposed to reach the whole world?

Genesis answers all of those questions. It doesn't answer them the way a textbook does, with bullet points and definitions. It answers them the way a story does, with people and places and choices and consequences that ripple across thousands of years.

And here's what might surprise you: it's not a boring story. Not even close.

WHAT YOU'RE ABOUT TO READ

Genesis covers more ground than any other book in the Bible. It stretches from the creation of the universe to a coffin in Egypt, from the first breath of the first human to the last words of a man named Joseph, spoken to his brothers in a foreign land. Thousands of years pass between the first verse and the last.

The book divides naturally into two major parts.

The first eleven chapters tell the story of the whole world. Creation. The fall. The first murder. A flood that wiped out nearly everything. A tower built by people who wanted to be their own gods. These chapters move fast, covering enormous stretches of time, and they explain how the world went from "very good" to very broken. By the end of chapter 11, humanity is scattered, divided by language, and far from God. Everything looks hopeless.

Then, in chapter 12, the camera zooms in. God calls one man, Abram, out of a pagan city and makes him a staggering promise: land, descendants, and a blessing that will eventually reach every nation on earth. The rest of Genesis follows that promise through four generations of one family: Abraham, Isaac, Jacob, and Joseph. It's a family saga full of faith and failure, love and rivalry, dreams and betrayals, and—running through all of it like a river—the relentless faithfulness of God.

You'll watch Abraham leave everything he knows and follow God into the unknown. You'll see him lie, stumble, and nearly lose the promise more than once. You'll stand with him on a mountain where God asks the unthinkable and then provides the unimaginable.

You'll meet Isaac, the miracle child who almost didn't survive, and Rebekah, the woman who said "I will go" to a servant she'd just met at a well.

You'll follow Jacob, the deceiver who stole a blessing, fled for his life, got cheated by his uncle, wrestled with God in the dark, and walked away limping with a new name and a new future.

And you'll watch Joseph go from his father's favorite to a pit to a slave market to a prison to the throne room of the most powerful nation on earth. His story is one of the most dramatic in all of literature, and its climax contains a sentence that might be the most important theological statement in the entire Old Testament: "You meant it for evil, but God meant it for good."

WHY THIS MATTERS

You might be wondering why a book written thousands of years ago about people in the ancient Near East matters to your life today.

It matters because the questions Genesis asks are the same questions you're asking.

Where did I come from? Genesis says you were made on purpose, by a God who called his creation "very good," and that you carry his image in a way nothing else in the universe does.

Why is the world so messed up? Genesis says it's because human beings chose their own way over God's way, and that choice fractured everything: our relationship with God, with each other, and with the world itself.

Does God care about me? Genesis says he does—fiercely. The God of Genesis isn't distant or detached. He walks in gardens. He makes clothes for the people who disobeyed him. He hears a slave woman crying in the desert. He remembers his promises when centuries pass without a word. He works through liars, cheaters, and cowards to accomplish things none of them could have imagined.

Can anything fix what's broken? Genesis says yes, but not quickly, and not the way you'd expect. The fix doesn't come through a flood that washes the world clean or a tower that reaches heaven. It comes through a promise, made to one man, carried through one family, and fulfilled, eventually, through one descendant who would bless every nation on earth.

That descendant is Jesus. Genesis doesn't name him. But it points to him on almost every page. The "seed" promised to Eve. The ram that replaced Isaac on the altar. The scepter that would not depart from Judah. The suffering servant who forgave his brothers and saved the world from starvation. Every major story in Genesis is casting a shadow toward someone who hadn't arrived yet.

BEFORE YOU START

A few things to keep in mind as you read.

Genesis is honest. The people in this book are not sanitized heroes. Abraham lies. Jacob cheats. Judah sells his own brother.

The women in the story are sometimes overlooked, sometimes mistreated, and sometimes the bravest people in the room. Genesis doesn't airbrush anyone. It shows real people with real failures being used by a real God whose plan doesn't depend on human perfection.

Genesis is sometimes hard. There's violence. There's family dysfunction that makes reality TV look tame. There are moments where God's actions raise questions that don't have easy answers. That's okay. The Bible doesn't ask you to stop thinking. It asks you to keep reading.

Genesis is the foundation. Almost every major idea in the rest of the Bible—sin, sacrifice, covenant, election, faith, redemption, the land, the seed, the blessing—starts here. If you understand Genesis, the rest of the Bible will make so much more sense. If you skip it, you'll be the person who walked into the movie late, trying to figure out what's in the briefcase.

LET'S BEGIN

So here we are, standing at the very first page of the very first book of the Bible. Behind us is nothing. Ahead of us is everything a universe spoken into existence, a garden planted by God's own hand, a man and a woman who had it all and threw it away, and a promise that will take the rest of Scripture to fulfill.

The first four words of the Bible are the most important sentence ever written. They tell you who is in charge, and they tell you that this story has a beginning, which means it's going somewhere.

"In the beginning, God."

Turn the page.

1

IN THE BEGINNING

If you've ever played *Minecraft* in creative mode, you know the feeling. You start with nothing but an empty world stretching out in every direction. No buildings. No farms. No villages. Just flat ground and open sky. And then you start building. You lay down blocks, shape the terrain, fill oceans with water, and plant forests wherever you want them. You can construct anything you can imagine, from a tiny cabin to a massive castle floating in the sky.

In *A Minecraft Movie*, a group of ordinary people gets pulled into the Overworld and discovers that this blocky universe has rules, structure, and purpose built into every layer of it. The world isn't random. Somebody designed it.

Now here's the difference between *Minecraft* and what you're about to read. In *Minecraft*, you build from materials that already exist. You mine stone. You chop wood. You smelt iron. Everything you create comes from something else. But when the Bible opens with the words, "In the beginning, God created the heavens and the earth," it's describing something no video game, no human being, and no force in the universe has ever done.

God didn't start with materials. He started with nothing. No blocks. No raw elements. No cosmic supply chest. Just God, and then his voice. He spoke, and the universe appeared.

That's where our story begins.

TEN WORDS THAT CHANGED EVERYTHING

The first verse of Genesis is one of the most famous sentences ever written: "In the beginning, God created the heavens and the earth." It sounds simple. It's only ten words in English. But those ten words make claims so enormous that people are still wrestling with them thousands of years later.

First, there was a beginning. Time itself had a starting point. There was a moment before which nothing existed except God.

Second, God was already there. He didn't come into being. He didn't evolve. He didn't have parents or a backstory. When everything else began, God simply *was*. The passage doesn't try to prove God exists. It doesn't argue for him. It just introduces him as the one who was there before anything else and who made everything else.

Third, he *created*. The word Moses used here is special. In the entire Old Testament, this particular word for "create" is only ever used with God as the one doing it. Humans can make things, build things, craft things. But this kind of creating, bringing something into existence out of absolutely nothing, belongs to God alone.

And what did he create? "The heavens and the earth." That's an ancient way of saying *everything*. The ground beneath your feet and the stars above your head. The oceans, the atmosphere, the galaxies you can see through a telescope and the ones you can't. All of it. Every atom, every particle, every corner of the universe owes its existence to this moment.

SIX DAYS: FROM CHAOS TO CREATION

What comes next is one of the most carefully structured passages in all of Scripture. Over six days, God transforms a dark, empty, formless world into a place teeming with life, beauty, and purpose.

Notice the pattern. The earth began "formless and empty," with darkness covering everything. So God spent the first three days giving it form, giving it shape and structure. Then he spent the next three days filling it, populating each space with the things it was designed to hold.

On the first day, God said, "Let there be light," and there was light. No delay. No effort. No spell or formula. Just a command, and reality obeyed. On the second day, he separated the waters, creating sky above and seas below. On the third day, he gathered the waters and let dry land appear, then covered it with plants and trees.

Then he filled what he'd formed. On the fourth day, the sun, moon, and stars. On the fifth day, birds for the sky and fish for the sea. On the sixth day, animals of every kind for the land.

Do you see the design? Days one through three build the rooms. Days four through six furnish them. Light gets its luminaries. Sky and sea get their creatures. Land gets its animals.

And over and over, like a drumbeat through the whole passage, you hear the same phrase: "And God saw that it was good." Not just acceptable. Not just functional. *Good.* God looked at what he made and was pleased with it. The light was good. The land was good. The plants, the fish, the animals, all good.

This matters more than you might think. In the ancient world, the nations surrounding Israel had their own stories about how the world began. In those stories, creation was usually born out of violence, gods fighting and killing each other, then using the leftovers to build the earth. Creation was an accident born out of chaos.

Genesis says the opposite. Creation wasn't an accident. It was the deliberate, joyful act of a God who spoke the universe into existence and then called it good.

THE CROWN OF CREATION

But the most important moment of creation wasn't the stars or the oceans or the mountains. It came on the sixth day, and it came with a pause.

For five and a half days, God had been creating by command. "Let there be light." "Let the waters be gathered." "Let the earth produce." But when he reached the final act of creation, the language shifted. Instead of a command directed outward, there was a conversation: "Let *us* make mankind in *our* image, in our likeness."

Something different was about to happen. Something personal. "So God created mankind in his own image, in the image of God he created them; male and female he created them."

Out of everything God made, only human beings received this designation. Not the stars. Not the mountains. Not the animals, as magnificent as they are. Only people were made in the image of God.

What does that mean? It doesn't mean we look like God physically, since God is spirit. It means something deeper. To be made in God's image means that human beings reflect God in ways nothing else in creation does. We can think, reason, create, and love. We have moral awareness, the ability to know the difference between right and wrong. We can have relationships, with each other and with God himself. We carry a dignity and a worth that comes not from what we can do but from whose image we bear.

And notice: God made humanity "male and female." Both bear his image equally. Both are essential. Both are part of God's design from the very beginning.

After creating human beings, God blessed them and gave them a job: "Be fruitful and increase in number; fill the earth and subdue it. Rule over the fish in the sea and the birds in the sky and over every living creature that moves on the ground." Humanity wasn't just placed in the world like a decoration. We were given responsibility. We were put in charge of caring for what God had made. We were meant to be his representatives on earth, managing his creation the way he would manage it, with wisdom, care, and purpose.

Then God looked at everything he had made, all six days of it, and this time the evaluation changed. It wasn't just "good."

It was *very* good.

THE GARDEN

Genesis 2 zooms in on the creation of humanity like a camera moving from a wide shot to a close-up. Chapter 1 gave us the big picture. Chapter 2 gives us the details.

God formed the first man from the dust of the ground and breathed into his nostrils the breath of life. Think about that image. God didn't just speak the man into existence from a distance. He got close. He shaped him like a potter working with clay. And then, in a moment of extraordinary intimacy, God leaned in and breathed life into him. The man's first breath came directly from the lungs of God.

This is personal. This is a Creator who isn't distant or detached. This is a God who gets his hands dirty, who bends down, who gives of himself to bring his creation to life.

God planted a garden in a place called Eden, a word that means "delight," and placed the man there to work it and take care of it. This wasn't slave labor. This was purpose. The man had a home, a mission, and a relationship with the God who made him. In the middle of the garden stood two trees that would matter more than any others: the tree of life and the tree of the knowledge of good and evil.

God gave the man one boundary: "You are free to eat from any tree in the garden; but you must not eat from the tree of the knowledge of good and evil, for when you eat from it you will certainly die." Freedom and limits. Blessing and warning. A whole garden full of "yes" and only one "no."

NOT GOOD TO BE ALONE

Then God said something surprising. After declaring everything good and even very good, he looked at the man alone and said, "It is not good for the man to be alone. I will make a helper suitable for him."

Not good. The only "not good" in the entire creation

account. The man by himself was incomplete. He needed someone who corresponded to him, someone who shared his nature, who could do what he could not do alone.

God brought every animal and bird to the man, and the man named them, an act that showed both authority and intelligence. But it also revealed a gap. For every creature that passed before him, there was no match. None of them shared his nature. None of them could be the partner he needed.

So God caused the man to fall into a deep sleep, took one of his ribs, and built a woman from it. When God brought her to the man, his response was immediate, joyful, and poetic. His very first recorded words in all of Scripture are a love poem: "This is now bone of my bones and flesh of my flesh; she shall be called 'woman,' for she was taken out of man."

At last. Someone like him. Someone who shared his nature, his dignity, his calling. The creation of humanity had reached its goal: man and woman together, equal in value, complementary in design, united in purpose.

Moses added an editorial note that echoes across the rest of the Bible: "That is why a man leaves his father and mother and is united to his wife, and they become one flesh." Marriage, the lifelong union of one man and one woman, wasn't a human invention. It was God's idea, established before sin entered the world, woven into the fabric of creation itself.

The chapter ends with an image of perfect peace: "Adam and his wife were both naked, and they felt no shame." No fear. No guilt. No hiding. Just two people living in the full light of God's presence, exactly as they were made to be.

It wouldn't last. But for now, it was very good.

WHAT THIS MEANS FOR US

First, you are not an accident. If Genesis 1 teaches us anything, it's that the universe was made on purpose, and you were made on purpose. You're not a random collection of cells that happened to come together by chance. You were designed by a God who wanted you to exist. That truth changes everything about how you see yourself and how you see other people.

Second, every person you meet bears the image of God. Not just the people you like. Not just the people who look, talk, or think like you. Every human being, regardless of age, race, ability, or background, carries the dignity of being made in God's image. That means bullying, cruelty, and looking down on others isn't just wrong because it's mean. It's an offense against the God whose image those people carry.

Third, God gave us work as a gift, not a punishment. Before sin ever entered the world, the man had a job. He was placed in the garden "to work it and take care of it." Work, using your talents and abilities to contribute something meaningful, is part of what it means to be human. It's not a curse. The curse came later, and it changed the nature of work. But the impulse to create, to build, to care for the world around you? That's from God.

Fourth, we were made for relationship. The only thing in all of creation that God called "not good" was the man being alone. You were not designed to go through life isolated. You need other people, and they need you. Friendship, family, community, these aren't optional add-ons to the human experience. They're built into the original design.

Fifth, freedom has boundaries, and that's a good thing. God gave Adam an entire garden full of trees to enjoy. The boundary wasn't there to limit his happiness. It was there to protect it. Every good thing in life comes with boundaries. When we respect them, things flourish. When we ignore them, things fall apart. As you'll see in the very next chapter, ignoring God's boundaries has consequences that reach far beyond what anyone expects.

TALKING POINTS

1. **God called his creation "good" six times and "very good" once.** What do you think it means that God considers his creation good? How should that shape the way we think about the natural world and our responsibility to take care of it?

2. **Being made in the "image of God" is what gives every human being value and dignity.** How does knowing this change the way you think about people who are different from you? How should it affect the way you treat people at school, online, or in your neighborhood?

3. **God gave Adam an entire garden full of "yes" and only one "no."** Why do you think people so often focus on the one thing they can't have instead of all the things they can? Do you ever find yourself doing that?

4. **The first thing God called "not good" was the man being alone.** Why do you think relationships are so important to God? What does it look like to be a good friend, a good family member, or a good part of your community?

5. **Genesis describes God creating in an orderly, purposeful way, six days of work followed by a day of rest.** What

does this tell us about how God values both work and rest? Do you think most people today have a healthy balance between the two?

The world is made. The garden is planted. The man and the woman stand together in the presence of God, naked and unashamed, surrounded by everything they could ever need. But there's a tree in the middle of the garden. And there's a serpent you haven't met yet.

Turn the page.

2

THE DAY EVERYTHING BROKE

In Mary Shelley's *Frankenstein*, a brilliant young scientist named Victor Frankenstein becomes obsessed with a question: What if I could create life? He has everything a person could want: a loving family, a future wife, and a promising career. But none of it is enough. He wants to cross a boundary no human being has ever crossed.

So he does. Alone in his laboratory, Victor stitches together a creature from dead tissue and brings it to life. The moment should be a triumph. Instead, it's a horror. The creature is hideous, and Victor abandons it. From that single act of grasping for something that didn't belong to him, everything unravels. The creature turns violent. One by one, everyone Victor loves is destroyed. His brother. His best friend. His wife. By the end of the story, Victor himself is dead.

Shelley's novel is about what happens when someone reaches beyond the boundaries they were given, not because the knowledge itself was evil, but because the reaching was an act of pride. Victor wanted to be God. And the consequences didn't stay contained. They spread outward, destroying everything they touched.

That's the story of Genesis 3. And chapters 4–5 show us just how far the destruction spread.

THE SERPENT'S QUESTION

At the end of Genesis 2, everything was perfect. The man and the woman stood in the garden, naked and unashamed, surrounded by God's generosity. They had one boundary: don't eat from the tree of the knowledge of good and evil.

Then the serpent showed up.

The Bible describes this creature as "more crafty than any of the wild animals the LORD God had made." He was shrewd. Cunning. And his strategy was devastatingly simple. He didn't start with a lie. He started with a question: "Did God really say, 'You must not eat from any tree in the garden'?"

Notice what the serpent did. God had said they could eat freely from *every* tree except one. The serpent twisted that into a question that made God sound stingy: "Did he really say you can't eat from *any* tree?" One small shift in emphasis, and suddenly God's generosity looked like restriction.

The woman corrected him, but she made her own subtle changes to God's command. She added "you must not touch it" and softened the certainty of death from "you will certainly die" to just "you will die." Small changes. But they show the command was already becoming blurry in her mind.

That's when the serpent dropped the lie: "You will not certainly die. For God knows that when you eat from it your eyes will be opened, and you will be like God, knowing good and evil."

Three moves. First, he contradicted God directly. Second, he questioned God's motives, implying that God was holding them back. Third, he offered them something that sounded incredible: you can be like God.

The serpent didn't show up with a pitchfork and a sign saying "Evil." He showed up with a question, a suggestion, and a half-truth that sounded reasonable. Temptation still works the same way.

THE BITE THAT CHANGED EVERYTHING

"When the woman saw that the fruit of the tree was good for food and pleasing to the eye, and also desirable for gaining wisdom, she took some and ate it. She also gave some to her husband, who was with her, and he ate it."

The whole thing happens in a single verse. After all the buildup, the actual sin takes barely a sentence. She saw. She took. She ate. She gave. He ate. That's it. That's how fast everything fell apart.

Notice that Adam was right there. The text says she gave it "to her husband, who was with her." He wasn't off somewhere else, tricked later by his wife. He was present. He watched. And he ate without a word of objection.

The results were immediate. "Then the eyes of both of them were opened, and they realized they were naked." The serpent had promised their eyes would be opened, and technically he was right. But what they saw wasn't divine wisdom. They saw their own shame. They sewed fig leaves together to cover themselves, and when they heard God walking in the garden, they hid.

Think about that. The two people who had walked freely in God's presence, who had nothing to fear and nothing to hide, were now crouching behind the trees, terrified of the God who made them.

Sin always promises more than it delivers. And it always costs more than you expect.

WHERE ARE YOU?

God came looking for them. Not because he didn't know where they were, but because he wanted them to come forward and own what they had done. "Where are you?" he called.

Adam's answer was honest but incomplete: "I heard you in the garden, and I was afraid because I was naked; so I hid."

God pressed further: "Have you eaten from the tree that I commanded you not to eat from?"

And here came the blame game. Adam pointed at Eve. "The woman you put here with me, she gave me some fruit from the tree, and I ate it." Did you catch that? He didn't just blame the woman. He blamed God for giving her to him.

God turned to the woman. "What is this you have done?" She pointed at the serpent. "The serpent deceived me, and I ate."

Everyone pointed somewhere else. But nobody could escape what they had done.

THE CONSEQUENCES

God addressed the guilty parties in reverse order, starting with the serpent. The serpent was cursed, sentenced to crawl on its belly, and placed in permanent conflict with humanity. But tucked inside that curse was something extraordinary: "I will put enmity between you and the woman, and between your offspring and hers; he will crush your head, and you will strike his heel."

This is the first promise of rescue in the entire Bible. Right here, in the middle of judgment, God announced that one day a descendant of the woman would crush the serpent's head. The serpent would land a blow, a strike to the heel, but the final victory would belong to the woman's offspring. It's a single verse, but the rest of the Bible is the story of that promise being fulfilled. Every generation after this one would live in the tension of that conflict, waiting for the one who would finally end it.

The woman's consequence touched her most intimate roles: pain in childbearing and conflict in her relationship with her husband. What had been designed for joy and partnership would now be marked by struggle.

The man's consequence struck at his daily work. The ground, which had freely produced everything he needed, was now cursed on his account. Thorns. Thistles. Sweat. Painful toil. And at the end of it all, death. "Dust you are and to dust you will return."

Notice: God cursed the serpent and the ground, but he did not curse the man or the woman. Judgment was real. Consequences were severe. But the blessing was not completely lost.

EAST OF EDEN

Even in judgment, God showed grace. He made garments of animal skin and clothed Adam and Eve, replacing the flimsy fig leaves they had stitched together with something that would actually protect them. This small act of provision meant something profound. God cared for them even after they had broken his command. And the fact that animals had to die to provide that covering was the first hint that the cost of dealing with sin would always involve innocent blood.

Then God drove them out of the garden. He stationed angelic beings at the entrance with a flaming sword to guard the way to the tree of life. Adam and Eve could no longer reach the tree that would have given them life forever. That sounds harsh, but consider: in a world now infected by sin, living forever might be more curse than blessing. God was protecting them even in their exile.

They left the garden and went east, away from God's presence, into a harder world. But they were alive. And the promise of 3:15 went with them.

BLOOD ON THE GROUND

Outside Eden, the first family began to grow. Eve gave birth to Cain, then Abel. Cain worked the soil. Abel kept flocks. Both brought offerings to God, but God accepted Abel's offering and rejected Cain's. Why?

The difference wasn't the type of offering, grain versus animal. The difference was the heart behind it. Abel brought the firstborn of his flock, the very best he had. The New Testament says he offered it "by faith" (Hebrews 11:4). Cain brought "some of the fruits of the ground," but nothing suggests it was his best, his first, or his finest. His offering cost him very little.

God confronted Cain directly: "If you do well, will you not

be accepted? And if you do not do well, sin is crouching at the door. Its desire is for you, but you must rule over it."

Cain had a choice. He could master the anger growing inside him, or he could let it master him.

He let it master him. Cain led his brother into a field and killed him. The first death in the Bible wasn't from old age or an accident. It was murder. Brother killing brother. The offspring of the serpent and the offspring of the woman were already at war, just as God had said.

When God asked, "Where is your brother?" Cain's response was defiant: "I don't know. Am I my brother's keeper?" No shame. No remorse. Just cold indifference.

God's answer was devastating: "Your brother's blood cries out to me from the ground." Cain was cursed and driven away, a restless wanderer. Yet even here, God showed mercy, placing a mark on Cain to protect him from being killed.

Sin was spreading. In the garden, it was a bite of fruit. Outside the garden, it was murder.

TWO FAMILY LINES

The rest of Genesis 4 and 5 trace what happened next through two very different family trees. Cain's descendants built cities, invented music, and developed metalworking. They achieved impressive things. But the line culminated in a man named Lamech, who boasted to his two wives about killing a man for merely wounding him. "If Cain is avenged seven times," Lamech bragged, "then Lamech seventy-seven times." Violence had gone from a single act of murder to a celebrated way of life. Technology advanced, but morality collapsed.

Then Genesis gives us Seth's line. After Abel's death, God gave Adam and Eve another son: Seth, whose name means "appointed." Through Seth, the promised line would continue. His descendants "began to call on the name of the LORD."

Genesis 5 traces Seth's family from Adam to Noah in a formal genealogy, and it has a rhythm you can't miss. Each entry follows the same pattern: he lived, he had sons and daughters, and then he died. Over and over, like a drumbeat: "And then he died. And then he died. And then he died." The curse of Genesis 3 was doing its work. Death was claiming every generation.

But one name broke the pattern. "Enoch walked faithfully with God; then he was no more, because God took him away." No death notice. No "and then he died." Enoch walked with God, and God simply took him. In the middle of a chapter dominated by death, one man's faithfulness showed that death didn't have to be the final word.

The chapter ends with the birth of Noah. His father Lamech (a different Lamech from Cain's line) named him Noah, meaning "rest" or "comfort," saying, "He will comfort us in the labor and painful toil of our hands caused by the ground the LORD has cursed." Noah's father longed for relief from the curse. He hoped his son might be the one to bring it.

He was right, in a way. But not in the way he expected.

WHAT THIS MEANS FOR US

First, take temptation seriously. The serpent didn't show up with a pitchfork and a sign saying "Evil." He showed up with a question, a suggestion, a half-truth that sounded reasonable. Temptation still works the same way. It rarely looks dangerous at first. It looks appealing, logical, and harmless. The best defense isn't willpower. It's knowing what God actually said and trusting that his boundaries are there to protect you, not to hold you back.

Second, understand that sin spreads. Adam and Eve's choice didn't stay contained. It leaked into their children, their grandchildren, and every generation after. One bite of fruit led to murder, then to boasting about murder, then to a world so corrupt that God would eventually grieve that he had made it. Sin is never just about you. It always affects the people around you.

Third, blame doesn't fix anything. Adam blamed Eve. Eve blamed the serpent. Cain denied everything. None of it changed what had happened. Owning your sin, honestly and without excuses, is the only path to forgiveness. God already knows what you've done. He's asking you to admit it, not so he can destroy you, but so he can begin to restore you.

Fourth, God's grace shows up in the darkest places. Clothing for the guilty. A mark of protection for a murderer. A new son to replace the one who was killed. Even in the middle of judgment, God kept providing, kept protecting, kept making a way forward. He has never stopped.

TALKING POINTS

1. **The serpent attacked God's character by suggesting God was holding Adam and Eve back.** Why do you think it's tempting to believe that God's rules are meant to limit us rather than protect us?

2. **When confronted, Adam blamed Eve and even blamed God.** Why is it so hard for people to own their mis-

takes? What happens in relationships when no one is willing to say, "I was wrong"?

3. **Cain's line produced cities, music, and metalworking, but also increasing violence.** How can good things like technology and art be used for evil? How do we make sure we're using our abilities for good?

4. **In a chapter full of death, Enoch "walked faithfully with God" and escaped it.** What do you think it means to "walk with God" in your everyday life? What would that look like at school, at home, or with your friends?

5. **God's first promise of rescue (Genesis 3:15) came in the middle of pronouncing judgment.** What does it tell us about God that his plan to save us was already in motion before Adam and Eve even left the garden?

The garden is behind them. The curse is real. Death is on the march. But a promise has been made, and that promise will not be broken. The question now is how bad things will get before they get better.

Turn the page.

3

THE FLOOD

In the movie *WALL·E*, the earth has become a garbage dump. Centuries of human carelessness have buried the planet under mountains of trash. The skies are brown. Nothing grows. The oceans are toxic. Humanity has fled to an enormous space cruiser called the Axiom, leaving behind a single robot, WALL·E, to compact the waste into cubes and stack them into skyscrapers of junk. The mission is supposed to take five years. It takes seven hundred.

When you first see earth in that movie, it's heartbreaking. This was supposed to be a beautiful world. You can tell it once was. But the creatures entrusted with caring for it ruined it instead, and the devastation is so total that the only solution is to start over.

That's essentially what happens in Genesis 6–9. God looked at the world he had made, the world he had called "very good," and saw that human wickedness had corrupted it beyond recognition. The violence was so pervasive, the evil so deep, that the Creator who had spoken the universe into existence decided to wipe the slate clean.

But not completely. Because in the middle of all that darkness, one man was still walking with God. And through that one man, God would preserve life and begin again.

EVERY INCLINATION, ONLY EVIL, ALL THE TIME

By the time we reach Genesis 6, the human race has been spiraling for generations. Cain murdered Abel. Lamech bragged about killing a man for wounding him. Sin, which had started as a single act of disobedience in a garden, had metastasized into a global epidemic.

Then comes one of the most devastating verses in the entire Bible: "The LORD saw how great the wickedness of the human race had become on the earth, and that every inclination of the thoughts of the human heart was only evil all the time." Read that again. *Every* inclination. *Only* evil. *All* the time.

This isn't a description of people who sometimes made bad choices. This is a portrait of a world where the human heart had been so thoroughly corrupted that goodness had nearly been extinguished. Violence filled the earth. The word used for that violence describes cold-blooded cruelty, the kind driven by greed and hate, with no regard for the fact that every victim bore the image of God.

And then the text says something startling: "The LORD regretted that he had made human beings on the earth, and his heart was deeply troubled." God wasn't indifferent to what had happened. He wasn't watching from a distance with detached irritation. He was grieved. The Creator's heart was broken over what his creation had become. The world he had spoken into existence with joy, the world he had called very good, had become a source of profound sorrow.

God decided to destroy what he had made. But tucked into the pronouncement of judgment was a single line of hope: "But Noah found favor in the eyes of the LORD."

A RIGHTEOUS MAN IN A WICKED WORLD

Noah stood out. He is described as "a righteous man, blameless among the people of his time," and he "walked with God." That phrase, "walked with God," had been used only once before in Genesis, to describe Enoch. In a world consumed by evil, Noah lived with integrity. He wasn't perfect, as we'll see later in the chapter. But his life was oriented toward God in a generation that had forgotten God entirely.

God told Noah what was coming. Unlike the flood stories of other ancient cultures, where the gods acted on a whim because humans were making too much noise, the God of Genesis explained *why* he was bringing judgment. The reason was moral. The earth was full of violence, and that violence was an assault on the image of God in every human being. God was not throwing a tantrum. He was executing justice.

But along with the announcement of destruction came a plan for rescue. God instructed Noah to build an ark, a massive, box-shaped barge roughly 450 feet long, 75 feet wide, and 45 feet high. To give you a sense of scale, that's longer than a football field and about four and a half stories tall. It had three decks, a door in the side, and an opening near the top. It had no sails and no rudder. There would be no steering this vessel. The fate of everyone on board would be entirely in God's hands.

Noah was told to bring his family and pairs of every kind of animal on board, along with enough food to sustain them all. And then comes one of the most quietly powerful sentences in Genesis: "Noah did everything just as God commanded him."

No argument. No negotiation. No delay. In a world that had abandoned God's word, one man still obeyed it.

THE WATERS RISE

When Noah was six hundred years old, the flood came. The text describes it as a catastrophic reversal of creation itself. Remember how God had separated the waters above from the waters below on the second day of creation? Now those boundaries collapsed. "All the springs of the great deep burst forth, and the floodgates of the heavens were opened." The architecture of creation was being dismantled. The separation that had made the world inhabitable was undone, and the waters rushed back in.

It rained for forty days and forty nights. The waters rose until they covered even the highest mountains. Everything that had the breath of life, every person, every animal, every bird, everything outside the ark, perished. The word used for "perished" is the same kind of language used elsewhere in the Bible for a person's last breath leaving their body. God, who had breathed life into creation, was now taking that breath back. It was the undoing of everything he had made.

Four times the text emphasizes that the waters "prevailed" over the earth. That word is a military term. The floodwaters were the army of the Lord, carrying out his judgment on a world that had filled itself with violence. The destruction was total.

And then comes the turning point: "But God remembered Noah."

GOD REMEMBERED

That sentence is the hinge on which the entire flood story turns. Everything before it describes destruction. Everything after it describes restoration. "God remembered Noah" doesn't mean God had forgotten about him, the way you might forget where you left your phone. In the Bible, when God "remembers" someone, it means he is about to act on their behalf. He is about to deliver.

God sent a wind over the earth, and the waters began to recede. The same word for "wind" is also the word for "spirit," the same word used in Genesis 1:2 when the Spirit of God hovered over the waters at creation. What was happening was nothing less than a new creation. God was doing again what he had done in the beginning, bringing order out of chaos, pushing back the waters, making the earth inhabitable once more.

The ark came to rest on the mountains of Ararat. Noah sent out a raven, then a dove, then another dove. The second dove came back with a fresh olive branch, a sign that plant life was returning to the earth. When the third dove didn't come back at all, Noah knew the land was dry.

After more than a year on the ark, God told Noah to come out. The language of disembarkation echoes the language of creation. God told the animals to "be fruitful and increase in number," the same blessing he had given at the beginning. Noah stepped off the ark onto a washed and renewed earth. It was, in effect, a second Genesis.

THE ALTAR AND THE PROMISE

The first thing Noah did on dry ground was build an altar and offer sacrifices to God. It was an act of worship and gratitude, an acknowledgment that his survival was not his own achievement but God's grace.

God's response is remarkable. He smelled the pleasing aroma of the sacrifice and made a promise: "Never again will I curse the ground because of humans, even though every inclination of the human heart is evil from youth. And never again will I destroy all living creatures, as I have done."

Notice something important. God made this promise *even though* the human heart hadn't changed. The flood wiped the earth clean, but it didn't fix the human problem. People after the flood would be just as prone to sin as people before it. God knew that. And he promised never to do this again anyway. The flood was a once-for-all demonstration of what sin deserves. But going forward, God would pursue a different strategy: not destruction but redemption.

God established a covenant with Noah, with his descendants, and with every living creature on earth. He promised that the natural order would continue: "As long as the earth endures, seedtime and harvest, cold and heat, summer and winter, day and night will never cease." The seasons would keep turning. Life would go on. God was committing himself to sustain the world he had remade.

And he gave a sign: the rainbow. The word used here is actually the word for a warrior's bow. Picture God hanging his weapon in the sky, pointed not at the earth but at himself, as if to say, "I swear on my own life that I will keep this promise." Every rainbow since has been a reminder that the God who judges is also the God who saves, and that his commitment to this world is unbreakable.

THE NEW WORLD AND ITS OLD PROBLEM

God blessed Noah and his family just as he had blessed Adam and Eve. "Be fruitful and increase in number and fill the earth." He gave them permission to eat meat for the first time, with the restriction that they must not eat the blood. And he established a rule that would protect the most fundamental truth about human beings: "Whoever sheds human blood, by humans shall their blood be shed; for in the image of God has God made mankind." Human life was sacred because every person still bore God's image. Violence against people was violence against God himself.

But the new world had the same old problem. Almost immediately, things started to go wrong.

Noah planted a vineyard, made wine, and got drunk. While he lay uncovered in his tent, his son Ham saw his father's nakedness and, instead of covering him, went and told his brothers about it. Shem and Japheth walked in backward and covered their father without looking. When Noah woke up and learned what Ham had done, he cursed Ham's son Canaan and blessed Shem and Japheth.

It's a strange and uncomfortable story. But its placement right after the flood is deliberate. It shows us that the problem of sin wasn't washed away by the waters. Noah, the one righteous man in his generation, was capable of failure. His own family was capable of dishonor. The flood had reset the world, but it hadn't reset the human heart.

The world needed more than a fresh start. It needed a Savior.

WHAT THIS MEANS FOR US

First, God takes sin seriously. The flood is a sobering reminder that God is not indifferent to evil. He sees it, he grieves over it, and there are consequences. The patience of God is real, but it is not infinite in every situation. The flood stands as a permanent warning that sin has a cost, and that cost can be catastrophic.

Second, grace always finds a way. Even in a world so corrupt that God determined to destroy it, he preserved one family. Even in judgment, he made a way of rescue. That pattern runs through the entire Bible, all the way to the cross. God never judges without also providing a door of escape for those who will trust him.

Third, obedience matters even when you're the only one. Noah built a massive boat in a world that had never seen a flood. He did it because God told him to, and he did it when no one else was listening. You will face moments in your life when doing the right thing makes you the odd one out. Noah's story says: do it anyway. God sees. God remembers. God delivers.

Fourth, a fresh start doesn't fix what's broken inside. The flood cleaned the earth, but it didn't cure the human heart. Noah himself proved that within a chapter. This is one of the most important lessons in all of Genesis: the problem isn't our circumstances. The problem is us. And the solution isn't a better environment. The solution is a God who can change us from the inside out. That's a solution only Jesus would ultimately provide.

TALKING POINTS

1. **Genesis 6:5 says that "every inclination of the thoughts of the human heart was only evil all the time."** What do you think the world looked like at that point? How does unchecked sin affect not just individuals but entire communities and cultures?

2. **Noah obeyed God when no one else around him was listening.** What makes it hard to do the right thing when everyone else is doing the wrong thing? Have you ever been in a situation like that?

3. **God promised never to flood the earth again, even though the human heart hadn't changed.** What does that tell you about how God has chosen to deal with sin going forward? Why do you think he chose patience and redemption over repeated destruction?

4. **The rainbow is described as a sign of God's covenant.** What's the difference between a sign and a decoration? How should we think about the rainbow when we see one?

5. **Noah's failure with the wine happened almost immediately after the flood.** What does this tell us about human nature? Why isn't a fresh start enough to solve the problem of sin?

The earth is clean. The covenant is made. The rainbow hangs in the sky. But the human heart is still restless, still prone to wander, still reaching for things that don't belong to it.

It won't be long before that restlessness builds a tower.

Turn the page.

4

THE TOWER AND THE NAME

In F. Scott Fitzgerald's *The Great Gatsby*, a mysterious million-aire named Jay Gatsby builds a colossal mansion on Long Island, throws lavish parties every weekend, and surrounds himself with hundreds of people. His house blazes with light. Music pours from every window. Everyone in New York knows his name.

But none of it is real. Gatsby built his empire for one reason: to be somebody. He grew up poor, and he spent his entire adult life constructing an identity grand enough to erase that past. The parties, the mansion, the reputation, all of it was an attempt to make a name for himself, to be remembered as something great.

It doesn't work. By the end of the novel, the parties are empty, the guests have vanished, and Gatsby is dead. The name he worked so hard to build dies with him. Everything he reached for slipped through his fingers. The famous last line of the book describes people like Gatsby as boats "borne back ceaselessly into the past," always straining forward but never arriving.

Genesis 11 tells the story of an entire civilization that tried to do what Gatsby did: make a name for themselves. They built something enormous. They reached for the heavens. And God brought it all crashing down.

SEVENTY NATIONS

Before we get to the tower, Genesis 10 pauses to give us something that might look boring at first glance: a genealogy. It's often called the Table of Nations, and it traces the descendants of Noah's three sons, Shem, Ham, and Japheth, as they spread across the ancient world. Seventy nations are listed, a number that in the Bible often symbolizes completeness. The point is that *all* the nations of the earth trace their origin back to one family, Noah's family, and ultimately to one Creator.

This matters more than you might think. In the ancient world, different nations worshiped different gods and assumed that other peoples had entirely separate origins. Genesis says no. Every nation, every tribe, every language group on earth shares a common ancestor and a common God. There is one human family.

The chapter also introduces a figure named Nimrod, described as "a mighty warrior on the earth." He founded some of the most famous cities of the ancient world, including Babylon and Nineveh. Keep Babylon in mind. It's about to become very important.

But Genesis 10 raises a question it doesn't answer. It describes the nations "each with its own language," spread across different territories. How did that happen? If everyone descended from Noah, why don't they all speak the same language?

Genesis 11 answers that question.

ONE LANGUAGE, ONE PLAN

"Now the whole world had one language and a common speech." That's how Genesis 11 opens. Everyone could understand everyone else. There were no translation barriers, no miscommunication, no division by dialect. Humanity was united.

The people migrated eastward, a direction that in Genesis often signals a move *away* from God. They settled on a plain in the land of Shinar, which is another name for Babylon. And there they made a plan.

"Come, let us make bricks. Come, let us build ourselves a city, with a tower that reaches to the heavens, so that we may make a name for ourselves; otherwise we will be scattered over the face of the whole earth."

Two things are happening here. First, they want to make a name for themselves. Sound familiar? God had told humanity to fill the earth, to spread out and populate it. Instead, they huddled together to build a monument to their own greatness. Only God has the right to make someone's name great, and he later promised to do exactly that for Abraham (12:2). But at Babel, people seized that privilege for themselves. It was the same impulse that drove Adam and Eve: reaching for what belongs to God.

Second, they were afraid. They didn't want to be scattered. They wanted to stay together, concentrated in one place, under one banner. On the surface, unity sounds like a good thing. But this was unity organized against God's purposes. It was unity built on pride and self-reliance, not on faith and obedience.

The tower itself was almost certainly a ziggurat, the kind of stepped pyramid common in ancient Mesopotamia. These structures were built as stairways between earth and heaven, places where the gods were supposed to descend. The builders of Babel weren't just constructing a tall building. They were trying to storm heaven itself.

THE LORD CAME DOWN

Here comes one of the most pointed moments in Genesis. The builders thought their tower was reaching the heavens. But the text says God had to *come down* just to see it.

Think about the irony. They built the tallest thing they could imagine, and from God's perspective, it was so small he had to stoop to look at it. Their grand project, the monument they believed would make them famous forever, was barely visible to the God who made the stars.

God assessed the situation and said, "If as one people speaking the same language they have begun to do this, then nothing they plan to do will be impossible for them." This wasn't a compliment. God wasn't impressed by their engineering. He was recognizing that a unified humanity, consumed by pride and turned away from him, was a dangerous thing. The last time wickedness had gone unchecked, it had required a flood. God would not let it reach that point again.

So he confused their language. The people who had come together with one speech suddenly couldn't understand each other. The construction project ground to a halt. The unity that had fueled their ambition dissolved into chaos. And the thing they feared most, being scattered across the face of the earth, happened anyway.

Moses, the author of Genesis, added a final jab. The

Babylonians claimed their city's name meant "gate of the gods." But in a pointed wordplay, Moses connected "Babel" with a word meaning "confused." The city that was supposed to be humanity's gateway to the heavens became the place where God turned their proud words into babble.

FROM SHEM TO ABRAM

After the tower falls and the nations scatter, Genesis 11:10–26 gives us one more genealogy. It traces a single line from Shem, Noah's son, all the way down to a man named Abram.

If you're paying attention, you'll notice something familiar. This genealogy has the same structure as the one in Genesis 5 that ran from Adam to Noah. Ten generations. The same pattern of fathers and sons. The same march of time. But one thing is different from Genesis 5: no one "walks with God." There is no Enoch. No standout. Just name after name, quietly narrowing the focus of the entire story from all the nations of the earth down to one family in one city in Mesopotamia.

And there's another change you might miss. The lifespans are dropping. In Genesis 5, people lived eight and nine hundred years. Here, the numbers decline rapidly. Shem lived six hundred years. By the time we get to Terah, Abram's father, the ages have fallen to just over two hundred. The curse of death is tightening its grip, generation by generation.

The genealogy ends with Terah fathering three sons: Abram, Nahor, and Haran. We learn that Haran died young. We learn that the family lived in Ur, a sophisticated city in Mesopotamia. And we learn one devastating detail about Abram's wife: "Sarai was barren; she had no children."

That detail is a bombshell. The entire book of Genesis has been building toward the fulfillment of God's promises through offspring, through "seed." And now the narrative zooms in on a man whose wife cannot have children. It looks like a dead end. How can God keep his promise of blessing through a barren couple in a pagan city?

The primeval history is over. The nations have been scattered. Languages have been confused. Sin is rampant. Death is universal. And the story has narrowed to a single, childless family in the middle of Mesopotamia.

Everything is about to change.

WHAT THIS MEANS FOR US

First, pride always overreaches. The builders of Babel wanted to be famous. They wanted to storm heaven. They wanted to control their own destiny. Instead, they lost everything they were trying to protect. That pattern repeats throughout history and throughout your own life. When we reach for glory that belongs to God, we don't become great. We become confused.

Second, God scatters what opposes him, but he gathers what belongs to him. Babel was scattered because its unity was built on rebellion. But later in the Bible, God would gather people from every nation and language into one family through faith. On the day of Pentecost, centuries later, God reversed Babel. People from every nation heard the gospel in their own language (Acts 2). What pride tore apart, the gospel puts back together.

Third, God's plan cannot be stopped. The nations scattered. Languages multiplied. Sin kept spreading. And yet, through all of it, God quietly preserved a single line of descent from Shem to Abram. His plan was never in jeopardy. It was narrowing to a point. And that point was about to become the most important calling in the history of the world.

TALKING POINTS

1. **The builders of Babel wanted to "make a name" for themselves.** Why do you think people are so driven to be famous or recognized? What's the difference between wanting to do something meaningful and wanting to be famous?

2. **God confused the languages at Babel, but on the day of Pentecost (Acts 2), he reversed it by letting people hear the gospel in their own language.** What does this tell us about God's ultimate plan for the nations?

3. **The genealogy in Genesis 11 quietly narrows the story from all the nations to one family.** Why do you think God chose to work through one family instead of fixing everything at once?

4. **Sarai was barren.** Why do you think Genesis draws attention to that detail right before the story of Abraham begins? What might God be setting up?

The nations are scattered. The languages are confused. The world is broken in ways a flood couldn't fix and a tower couldn't solve. But in a city called Ur, there's a man named Abram. He doesn't know it yet, but God is about to speak to him. And when he does, everything changes.

Turn the page.

5

THE MAN WHO LEFT EVERYTHING

In Charles Dickens' *Great Expectations*, a poor orphan boy named Pip is living a quiet, unremarkable life in a small English village. He works at his brother-in-law's blacksmith forge. He has no money, no prospects, and no reason to expect anything will ever change. Then one day a lawyer shows up with staggering news: a mysterious benefactor has chosen Pip to receive a fortune. He will be educated, given wealth, and transformed into a gentleman. But there's a catch. He has to leave. He has to walk away from the forge, from Joe the blacksmith who raised him, from every familiar thing in his small world, and go to London to begin a life he can barely imagine.

Pip goes. He leaves behind the only home he's ever known, carried forward by the promise of a benefactor he's never met. The journey changes him, not always for the better. He makes mistakes. He grows proud. He looks down on the people who loved him. But the promise is real, even when Pip doesn't deserve it, and the story of how that promise unfolds is far stranger and more painful than anything he expected.

Genesis 12 tells the story of a man who received a similar summons. His name was Abram, and his mysterious benefactor was God himself. The promise wasn't wealth or status. It was something far greater: a land, a family, and a blessing that would reach every nation on earth. But to receive it, Abram had to leave everything behind.

A BARREN BEGINNING

The story of Abram begins with a problem. At the end of Genesis 11, we learn that his father, Terah, lived in Ur of the Chaldeans, a sophisticated city in Mesopotamia. Terah had three sons: Abram, Nahor, and Haran. Haran died young. The family eventually migrated to the city of Haran, where they settled.

Then comes the detail that sets up everything: "Now Sarai was barren; she had no children." That single sentence is a bombshell. The entire book of Genesis has been tracking God's plan to bless the world through offspring, through a promised line of descendants stretching from Adam to Seth to Noah to Shem. And now the narrative zooms in on a man whose wife cannot have children. The pipeline of promise appears to be sealed shut.

This is where God does what God does best. He walks straight into an impossible situation and makes a promise.

GO

"The LORD had said to Abram, 'Leave your country, your people and your father's household and go to the land I will show you.'"

Think about what God was asking. In the ancient world, your identity was built on three things: your land, your people, and your father's house. That was your security, your inheritance, your place in the world. God told Abram to leave all three. Walk away from your country. Walk away from your community. Walk away from your family's estate. Go to a place I haven't told you about yet. No map. No coordinates. No timeline. Just "go."

But the command came packaged with promises, seven of them: "I will make you into a great nation, and I will bless you; I will make your name great, and you will be a blessing. I will bless those who bless you, and whoever curses you I will curse; and all peoples on earth will be blessed through you."

There are four big promises buried in those words. First, property: God would give Abram a land. Second, posterity: God would make his descendants into a great nation. Third, prosperity: God would bless him and make his name great. Fourth, protection: anyone who cursed Abram would face God's judgment.

And the purpose of it all? "All peoples on earth will be blessed through you." This wasn't just about one man's family. This was God's answer to the mess of Genesis 3–11. Sin had fractured the world. The nations had been scattered at Babel. Now God was choosing one man through whom he would begin putting everything back together.

Notice something: at Babel, people tried to "make a name" for themselves and failed. Here, God promises to make Abram's name great. The glory they seized, God would freely give.

"So Abram left, as the LORD had told him." He was seventy-five years old. He took Sarai and his nephew Lot, packed everything he owned, and headed for a land he had never seen.

That's faith. Not perfect understanding. Not a complete picture. Just trusting God enough to take the next step.

CRACKS IN THE FAITH

When Abram arrived in Canaan, God appeared to him and added a new layer to the promise: "To your offspring I will give this land." Abram built an altar and worshiped. It was a high point.

It didn't last. A famine hit the land. Canaan, the place God had just promised him, couldn't feed his family. So Abram went down to Egypt. And the moment he crossed the border, fear took over. Sarai was beautiful, and Abram was convinced the Egyptians would kill him to take her. So he told her to say she was his sister.

It was a half-truth. Sarai was a relative. But the intent was pure deception, and it put Sarai in terrible danger. Pharaoh took her into his household. Abram received livestock and servants as a bride price. Everything about the arrangement was wrong.

But God intervened. He struck Pharaoh's household with plagues, severe enough that Pharaoh figured out what had happened. He confronted Abram: "What have you done to me? Why didn't you tell me she was your wife?" Then he expelled Abram from Egypt.

It's an uncomfortable story. The man God just called to bless the nations is lying to a pagan king, and the pagan king comes out looking more honorable than Abram. But that's one of the things Genesis does so honestly. It doesn't pretend its heroes are perfect. It shows us real people with real failures being used by a God whose plan doesn't depend on their flawlessness.

And there's an echo here that Moses' original readers would have caught. Abram goes down to Egypt because of famine, his wife is taken, God sends plagues on the Egyptians, and Abram comes out wealthy. Centuries later, the entire nation of Israel would follow the same path: down to Egypt because of famine, enslaved, delivered by plagues, and leaving with Egyptian wealth. Abram's story was a preview of what was coming for his descendants.

THE SEPARATION

Back in Canaan, a new problem surfaced. Abram and Lot had both become so wealthy that the land couldn't support them both. Their herdsmen quarreled over resources.

Abram handled it with remarkable generosity. "Let's not have any quarreling between you and me," he said. "Is not the whole land before you? If you go to the left, I'll go to the right; if you go to the right, I'll go to the left." He gave Lot first pick.

Lot looked toward the Jordan plain and saw that it was lush, well-watered, "like the garden of the LORD." So he chose it. He moved east, toward the cities of Sodom and Gomorrah. The text makes sure we know what he was walking into: "Now the people of Sodom were wicked and were sinning greatly against the LORD."

Lot chose with his eyes. Abram trusted with his faith. After Lot left, God spoke again: "Look around from where you are, to the north and south, to the east and west. All the land that you see I will give to you and your offspring forever. I will make your offspring like the dust of the earth." Abram had given away the best portion, and God responded by promising him everything.

WARRIOR AND WORSHIPER

Genesis 14 takes an unexpected turn. Four eastern kings invaded the region, defeated the kings of Sodom and its allied cities, and carried off plunder and captives, including Lot. When Abram heard about it, he armed 318 trained men from his household, pursued the invaders, and defeated them in a night raid, rescuing Lot, the other captives, and all the stolen goods.

It's the only time in Genesis that Abram acts as a military commander. And immediately afterward, two kings come out to meet him.

The first is Melchizedek, king of Salem and "priest of God Most High." He brought bread and wine, blessed Abram, and declared that God Most High had delivered Abram's enemies into his hand. Abram gave Melchizedek a tenth of everything he had recovered.

The second was the king of Sodom, who offered Abram a deal: keep the plunder for yourself and just return my people. Abram refused. "I have raised my hand to the LORD, God Most High, Creator of heaven and earth, and have taken an oath that I will accept nothing belonging to you. I will not have you saying, 'I made Abram rich.'"

Two responses to the same victory. Abram worshiped the God who gave him the victory and refused to profit from a king whose city was infamous for its wickedness. His wealth would come from God, not Sodom.

COUNTED AS RIGHTEOUS

After these events, God came to Abram in a vision. "Do not be afraid, Abram. I am your shield, your very great reward."

Abram's response was honest and a little raw. "Sovereign LORD, what can you give me since I remain childless?" Years had passed since the original promise. Sarai was still barren. Abram was looking at a servant named Eliezer as his only heir. The promise of descendants as numerous as the dust of the earth must have felt like a cruel joke.

God answered by taking Abram outside. "Look up at the sky and count the stars, if indeed you can count them. So shall your offspring be."

And then comes one of the most important sentences in the entire Old Testament: "Abram believed the LORD, and he credited it to him as righteousness."

Abram had not earned righteousness by perfect behavior. His record in Egypt alone proved that. But he trusted God. He believed that what God promised, God would do. And God counted that faith, that trust, as righteousness. This verse became the foundation for the New Testament's teaching that we are made right with God not by being perfect but by trusting in his promises (Romans 4:3; Galatians 3:6).

Then God sealed the deal. He instructed Abram to prepare an ancient covenant ceremony: animals cut in half, arranged in two rows, with a path between them. In the ancient world, both parties in a covenant would walk between the pieces, essentially saying, "May what happened to these animals happen to me if I break this promise."

But when darkness fell and Abram waited, only God passed through. A smoking firepot and a blazing torch, symbols of God's presence, moved between the pieces. Abram didn't walk through. God took the entire obligation on himself.

This covenant wasn't a two-sided contract. It was a one-sided promise. God was staking his own life on it.

In that moment, God also revealed the future: Abram's descendants would be strangers in a foreign country and enslaved for four hundred years. But God would judge that nation, and Abram's people would come out with great possessions. The land of Canaan would be theirs. The promise was sure.

WHAT THIS MEANS FOR US

First, God calls ordinary people into extraordinary stories. Abram wasn't a king, a prophet, or a priest when God found him. He was a man from a pagan city with a barren wife. God doesn't wait for you to be impressive before he uses you. He calls you as you are and then shapes you along the way.

Second, faith is not the absence of failure. Abram lied in Egypt. He stumbled. But his failures didn't cancel God's promises. If God only worked through people who never made mistakes, he would never work through anyone. What mattered was that Abram kept believing, kept trusting, kept getting back up.

Third, God's promises require patience. Abram waited years for a child that never came during these chapters. The promise of land and descendants seemed impossible. But God's timing is not our timing. He is never late, even when it feels like he is. If you are waiting on God for something, Abram's story is a reminder that waiting is not the same as being forgotten.

Fourth, real faith means trusting God with what you can't see. Abram left his country without a map. He looked at an empty sky and believed it would be filled with his descendants.

He watched a firepot pass through the darkness and trusted that God's promise was sure. That's the kind of faith God credits as righteousness. Not perfection. Trust.

TALKING POINTS

1. **God asked Abram to leave his country, his people, and his father's house.** What would be the hardest thing for you to leave behind if God asked you to go somewhere new? Why?

2. **Abram's failure in Egypt didn't cancel God's promises.** How does knowing this affect the way you think about your own mistakes? Does God give up on people who stumble?

3. **Abram gave Lot first choice of the land and trusted God with whatever was left.** Why is it hard to be generous when something valuable is at stake? What happens when we trust God instead of fighting for the best position?

4. **God "credited" Abram's faith as righteousness.** What does it mean that God values our trust more than our performance? How should that change the way we approach our relationship with him?

5. **In the covenant ceremony, only God passed between the pieces.** What does it tell us about God that he took the entire obligation on himself? How does that point forward to what Jesus did for us?

The promise has been made. The covenant has been cut. Abram has been declared righteous by faith. But Sarai's womb is still empty, and the temptation to take matters into their own hands is about to prove irresistible.

Turn the page.

6

WHEN WAITING BECOMES TOO MUCH

In Disney's *Pinocchio*, an old woodcarver named Geppetto wishes on a star for his puppet to become a real boy. A fairy grants the wish, sort of. She brings Pinocchio to life, but he isn't a real boy yet. He has to earn it. "Prove yourself brave, truthful, and unselfish," she tells him, "and someday you will be a real boy." In the meantime, she assigns a cricket named Jiminy to be his conscience.

It should be simple. Go to school. Do the right thing. Wait for the promise to come true. But Pinocchio can't wait. On his very first day, he's lured off the path by a fox and a cat who promise him fame and fortune without any of the hard work. One shortcut leads to another. He ends up on Pleasure Island, a place that looks like paradise but turns boys into donkeys. By the time Pinocchio realizes what's happening, the consequences are already closing in, and the person who suffers most is Geppetto, who goes searching for his lost son and ends up swallowed by a whale.

The whole movie is about what happens when you refuse to wait for a promise the right way. Pinocchio wanted to be real, and the path was there. But the waiting felt too slow, the shortcuts looked too good, and the cost of impatience fell hardest on the people who loved him most.

Genesis 16–18 tells a strikingly similar story. A couple had been promised a son. Years passed. Nothing happened. So they took a shortcut. The results were painful, messy, and far-reaching. But God was not done. He never is.

SARAI'S PLAN

It had been ten years since Abram arrived in Canaan. Ten years since God promised descendants as numerous as the stars. And Sarai's womb was still empty.

Her frustration was raw and honest: "The LORD has kept me from having children." She wasn't wrong. The Bible itself acknowledged that her barrenness was from God. But instead of bringing her pain to the God who had caused it, Sarai devised a plan of her own. "Go, sleep with my maidservant," she told Abram. "Perhaps I can build a family through her."

This wasn't as shocking in the ancient world as it sounds to us. It was common practice for a barren wife to give her servant to her husband as a surrogate. Legal codes in the ancient Near East even regulated the arrangement and its consequences. Culturally, Sarai was doing what any desperate woman of her time might do.

But this isn't just a cultural story. It's a spiritual one. And the way Moses tells it, the echoes of Eden are impossible to miss. Sarai "took" Hagar and "gave" her to her husband. Those are the same words used when Eve "took" the fruit and "gave" it to Adam. Abram "agreed to what Sarai said," the same language used when God condemned Adam for listening to his wife instead of obeying God's word. The pattern is unmistakable: once again, a husband and wife are taking what belongs to God's timing into their own hands.

Abram was passive. The warrior who had charged into battle against four kings to rescue Lot now stood silent as his wife rearranged God's plan. He didn't pray. He didn't protest. He didn't remind Sarai of the promise. He just went along with it.

The plan worked, technically. Hagar became pregnant. But the moment she did, everything fell apart. Hagar began to look down on Sarai. Sarai, furious, blamed Abram. Abram, still passive, told Sarai to handle it herself. And Sarai treated Hagar so harshly that the pregnant servant fled into the desert.

One shortcut. One moment of impatience. And now the household was in ruins.

THE GOD WHO SEES

Hagar was alone in the wilderness, pregnant and afraid, heading back toward Egypt with nothing. She had been used, mistreated, and discarded. No one in the household had even called her by name. To Abram and Sarai, she was just "my servant" or "your servant."

But God found her. The angel of the Lord appeared to Hagar at a spring in the desert and called her by name. "Hagar, servant of Sarai, where have you come from, and where are you going?"

It was a gentle question, not an accusation. God knew the answer. He wanted Hagar to say it out loud.

The angel told her to go back and submit to Sarai, which

must have been an incredibly difficult command. But he also gave her a promise: "I will increase your descendants so much that they will be too numerous to count." He told her to name her son Ishmael, meaning "God hears," because the Lord had heard her in her misery. Her son would be wild and independent, living on the fringes of civilization, a fighter who would hold his own against everyone.

Hagar's response is one of the most beautiful moments in Genesis. She gave God a name: "You are the God who sees me." In a world where she was invisible, where she had been treated as a tool, God saw her. He knew her name. He knew her pain. He had a plan for her son.

This is the first time in the Bible that a human being gives God a name. And it came not from a patriarch or a prophet but from an Egyptian slave woman crying in the desert. God's concern for the overlooked, the outcast, and the powerless is written into the earliest pages of Scripture.

Hagar went back. She submitted to a hard situation because she trusted the God who saw her. And she gave birth to Ishmael. Abram was eighty-six years old. He finally had a son, but not the son God had promised.

NEW NAMES, NEW PROMISE

Thirteen years of silence followed. Thirteen years in which Abram likely assumed Ishmael was the answer. Thirteen years in which God said nothing.

Then, when Abram was ninety-nine years old, the LORD appeared to him again and said, "I am God Almighty; walk before me faithfully and be blameless." God was reaffirming the covenant, but this time he added something new: obligations. Abram was called not just to believe but to live in a way that reflected that belief.

God also did something deeply personal. He changed their names. Abram, meaning "exalted father," became Abraham, meaning "father of many." Sarai became Sarah. Both names pointed to the same impossible future: this elderly, childless couple would be the parents of nations and kings.

As the sign of the covenant, God instituted circumcision. Every male in Abraham's household was to be circumcised as a physical reminder that they belonged to God and that God's promises would be carried forward through their descendants.

When God specifically said that Sarah, not Hagar, would bear the promised son, Abraham's reaction was blunt. He "fell facedown and laughed." Then he said, "Will a son be born to a man a hundred years old? Will Sarah bear a child at the age of ninety?" He even tried to redirect: "If only Ishmael might live under your blessing!"

God's response was firm. He would bless Ishmael and make him into a great nation, but the covenant would be established through Isaac, the son Sarah would bear within a year. The name Isaac means "he laughs," a permanent reminder that both Abraham and Sarah had laughed at the impossibility of God's plan.

Abraham obeyed. That very day, he circumcised every male in his household, including thirteen-year-old Ishmael and himself at ninety-nine. Whatever doubts he had, his obedience was immediate.

THREE VISITORS

Not long after, Abraham was sitting at the entrance to his tent in the heat of the day when he looked up and saw three men standing nearby. He didn't know who they were, but he treated them with extraordinary generosity. He ran to greet them, bowed to the ground, and begged them not to pass by. He rushed to prepare a feast: fresh bread, a choice calf, curds, and milk. He stood nearby while they ate, serving them personally.

One of these visitors was the Lord himself, accompanied by two angels. Abraham didn't fully realize this at first, but the conversation that followed made it unmistakable.

"Where is your wife Sarah?" the visitor asked. That question alone should have been a clue. How did a stranger know her new name?

Then came the announcement: "I will surely return to you about this time next year, and Sarah your wife will have a son."

Sarah was listening from inside the tent. And she laughed. Not the laugh of joy. The laugh of a woman who had stopped hoping a long time ago. She thought to herself, "After I am worn out and my lord is old, will I now have this pleasure?"

The Lord turned to Abraham and asked a question that echoes through the rest of the Bible: "Why did Sarah laugh? Is anything too hard for the LORD? I will return to you at the appointed time next year, and Sarah will have a son."

Sarah, afraid, denied laughing. "I did not laugh," she said. The Lord's reply was simple and final: "Yes, you did laugh."

It wasn't a rebuke so much as a gentle correction. God wasn't angry at Sarah for doubting. He was insisting that she hear the truth: this was going to happen, whether she believed it or not.

The God who created the universe by speaking it into existence was not going to be stopped by old age. The promise had an "appointed time." It was fixed. It was certain. And it was coming.

WHAT THIS MEANS FOR US

First, shortcuts around God's plan always cost more than you expect. Sarai's decision to use Hagar seemed practical, even culturally acceptable. But it created a wound in Abraham's family that never fully healed. When we get tired of waiting on God and try to manufacture our own answers, we almost always create problems that are harder to solve than the one we were trying to fix. Patience is not passive. It's the active decision to trust God's timing over your own.

Second, God sees the people the world overlooks. Hagar was a foreign slave with no power and no voice. But God found her in the desert, called her by name, and gave her a future. If you have ever felt invisible, ignored, or forgotten, Hagar's story is for you. The God of the Bible is not just the God of the powerful and the prominent. He is the God who sees.

Third, God's promises don't expire. Thirteen years of silence between chapters 16 and 17 must have felt like an eternity. But God hadn't forgotten. He hadn't changed his mind. He was working on his own timetable, which is always better than ours. If you're waiting on something you've been praying about for a long time, don't confuse God's silence with God's absence.

Fourth, nothing is too hard for the Lord. That question from Genesis 18:14 deserves to be written on the wall of your room. Whatever you're facing, whatever seems impossible, whatever makes you want to laugh the way Sarah laughed,

God is not limited by your circumstances. He specializes in doing what can't be done.

TALKING POINTS

1. **Sarai's plan to use Hagar was culturally acceptable but spiritually disastrous.** Can you think of situations today where something might be "normal" or accepted by society but still not what God wants? How do you tell the difference?

2. **God called Hagar by name when everyone else treated her as invisible.** Why do you think it matters so much to be known and seen? How can you be someone who "sees" the overlooked people in your school, neighborhood, or church?

3. **Abraham laughed when God promised a son.** Sarah laughed too. Yet God wasn't offended. He named the child "he laughs." What does that tell you about how God responds to our doubts? Does doubt disqualify us from God's plan?

4. **God was silent for thirteen years between chapters 16 and 17.** Have you ever felt like God was silent in your life? How do you keep trusting when you can't hear anything?

5. **"Is anything too hard for the LORD?"** What is one thing in your life right now that feels impossible? How does this question change the way you think about it?

The son of promise has been announced. Sarah will bear a child within a year. But before that child arrives, Abraham will stand before God and argue for the lives of strangers in a doomed city. And his nephew Lot is about to learn what happens when you pitch your tent too close to Sodom.

Turn the page.

7

FIRE FROM HEAVEN

In Harper Lee's *To Kill a Mockingbird*, a lawyer named Atticus Finch agrees to defend a Black man named Tom Robinson who has been falsely accused of a crime in 1930s Alabama. Atticus knows the town. He knows the jury. He knows the verdict is almost certainly already decided before the trial begins. The whole system is rigged against an innocent man, and the guilty will walk free.

But Atticus shows up anyway. He stands in the courtroom and makes his case, not because he thinks he'll win, but because it's right. Because someone has to stand between the innocent and the mob. Because justice matters, even when injustice is going to carry the day.

There's a moment near the end of the trial when Atticus makes his closing argument. He looks at the jury and says, in effect: you know what is right. The question is whether you'll do it. The whole courtroom holds its breath. And then the verdict comes back guilty, and the innocent man is condemned.

Genesis 18–19 tells a story with some of the same tension. Abraham stands before God and argues for the innocent in a city full of wickedness. God listens. God agrees. But when the investigation is over, there aren't enough righteous people to save the city. And fire falls from heaven.

THE NEGOTIATION

After the three visitors announced that Sarah would have a son, two of them headed toward Sodom. But the Lord lingered with Abraham. And then came a remarkable moment. God decided to let Abraham in on what was about to happen.

Why? Because Abraham had been chosen to be a channel of blessing to all nations. Because God intended for Abraham to teach his descendants "to do what is right and just." And because Abraham, as the first intercessor in the Bible, needed to understand something about the God he served: that God is both perfectly just and extraordinarily merciful, and that those two qualities exist in a tension only God can resolve.

God told Abraham that the outcry against Sodom and Gomorrah was "so great" and their sin "so grievous" that he was going to investigate personally. The word "outcry" is significant. In the Bible, it describes the cries of victims suffering injustice, the screams of the oppressed, the pleas of people who have no one to defend them. Sodom's sin wasn't just offensive to polite society. It was generating the kind of suffering that reaches heaven.

Abraham understood what was coming. And he stepped forward.

"Will you sweep away the righteous with the wicked?" he asked. "What if there are fifty righteous people in the city? Will you really sweep it away and not spare the place for the sake of the fifty righteous people in it? Far be it from you to do such a thing, to kill the righteous with the wicked. Far be it from you! Will not the Judge of all the earth do right?"

That last question is one of the most important in the entire Bible. Abraham wasn't questioning whether God had the power to destroy Sodom. He was asking whether God's justice could be trusted. If the righteous are destroyed alongside the wicked, what kind of judge is God?

The Lord agreed. If fifty righteous people could be found, he would spare the city.

Abraham pressed further. Forty-five? Forty? Thirty? Twenty? Ten?

Each time, God agreed. For the sake of ten righteous people, God would not destroy Sodom. Abraham stopped at ten. He didn't go lower. Perhaps he assumed that Lot's family, at minimum, would account for that number.

He assumed wrong.

THE NIGHT SODOM FELL

The two angels arrived in Sodom that evening. Lot was sitting at the city gate, a sign that he held some position of influence in the community. When he saw the visitors, he bowed and urged them to spend the night at his house. They initially declined, planning to sleep in the town square. But Lot insisted. He knew what happened to strangers in Sodom after dark.

That night, every man in the city, young and old, surrounded Lot's house. They demanded that Lot bring out his guests so they could assault them. The mob's intent was violent and sexual, a grotesque violation of the most basic standards of hospitality and human decency. Sodom's sin, as the prophets later described it, was a toxic combination of sexual perversion, arrogance, cruelty, and indifference to the vulnerable (Ezekiel 16:49–50). The scene at Lot's door was the final confirmation of what the outcry had already announced: the city was beyond rescue.

Lot tried to reason with the mob. He even made a desperate, disturbing offer of his own daughters, an act that reveals how deeply the moral rot of Sodom had infected even the one "righteous" man living there (2 Peter 2:7–8). The mob refused and turned on Lot himself: "This fellow came here as a foreigner, and now he wants to play the judge!"

The angels pulled Lot inside, struck the mob with blindness, and delivered the verdict: "We are going to destroy this place. The outcry to the LORD against its people is so great that he has sent us to destroy it."

Lot tried to warn his sons-in-law. They laughed. They thought he was joking.

At dawn, the angels grabbed Lot, his wife, and his two daughters by the hand and dragged them out. Even then, Lot hesitated. The text says the angels "grasped his hand" because "the LORD was merciful to them." Left to himself, Lot would have died in Sodom. He was saved not by his own wisdom or courage but by the mercy of God reaching down and physically pulling him out.

The angels told them to flee to the mountains and not look back. Lot begged for permission to escape to a nearby small town called Zoar instead. The request was granted.

Then the fire fell. "The LORD rained down burning sulfur on Sodom and Gomorrah, from the LORD out of the heavens."

The cities, the entire plain, every living thing in the area was destroyed. The lush, well-watered land that had once looked "like the garden of the LORD" was reduced to smoke and ash.

And Lot's wife looked back. She became a pillar of salt. Jesus would later use her as a warning: "Remember Lot's wife" (Luke 17:32). Looking back at what God has judged is more than nostalgia. It's a heart that hasn't fully left.

The next morning, Abraham stood at the place where he had pleaded with God and looked toward Sodom. All he could see was dense smoke rising from the plain, "like smoke from a furnace." His intercession had not saved the city. There weren't even ten righteous people.

But the text adds a quiet note: "When God destroyed the cities of the plain, he remembered Abraham, and he brought Lot out of the catastrophe." Lot was saved not because of his own merit but because God remembered Abraham. The intercessor's prayer had not gone unheard. It just didn't look the way Abraham expected.

AFTER THE FIRE

The aftermath of Sodom's destruction is one of the darkest passages in Genesis. Lot and his two daughters ended up hiding in a cave in the mountains. The daughters, believing that no men were left to marry them, got their father drunk on successive nights and slept with him. Each became pregnant. The older daughter's son was Moab, father of the Moabites. The younger daughter's son was Ben-Ammi, father of the Ammonites.

Genesis tells this without commentary, without excusing or explaining. It simply shows us the wreckage. A man who had pitched his tent toward Sodom, who had moved inside its gates, who had been dragged out by angels, was now living in a cave while his daughters committed incest. The moral contamination of Sodom had followed Lot out of the city. You can leave a place, but if the place is inside you, leaving isn't enough.

THE SAME MISTAKE, AGAIN

You might think that after watching Sodom burn, Abraham would never repeat the fear-driven deception that got him in trouble in Egypt. You would be wrong.

In Genesis 20, Abraham moved to the region of Gerar, and once again told the local king, Abimelech, that Sarah was his sister. Once again, the king took Sarah into his household. Once again, Abraham chose self-preservation over honesty, putting Sarah and the promise in danger.

But this time, God intervened before any harm was done. He appeared to Abimelech in a dream and told him bluntly: "You are as good as dead because of the woman you have taken; she is a married woman." Abimelech, who had acted in innocence, protested. God acknowledged his innocence but told him it was God himself who had kept the king from sinning. "Now return the man's wife," God said, "for he is a prophet, and he will pray for you and you will live."

The next morning, Abimelech confronted Abraham. "What have you done to us? What was your reason for doing this?" Abraham's explanation was weak: "I said to myself, 'There is surely no fear of God in this place, and they will kill me because of my wife.'" He also admitted that the deception was a longstanding arrangement: "Everywhere we go, I say of her, 'He is my brother.'"

It's a humbling scene. A pagan king acted with more integrity than the father of the faithful. Abimelech returned Sarah, gave Abraham livestock and servants, offered him land, and paid a thousand shekels of silver to settle the matter publicly. Then Abraham prayed for Abimelech, and God healed the king's household. The Lord had closed the wombs of every woman in Abimelech's house on account of Sarah, and Abraham's intercession reversed it.

The episode is uncomfortable for the same reason it's important. Genesis does not airbrush its hero. Abraham was a man of genuine, extraordinary faith, but he was also capable of falling into the same trap twice. The same man who stood before God and argued for the righteous at Sodom was the same man who lied about his wife to save his own skin. Both things were true. Both things are true of every person who has ever tried to follow God.

And yet God's plan moved forward anyway. Sarah was protected. The promise was intact. The child would come. Not because Abraham was flawless but because God was faithful.

WHAT THIS MEANS FOR US

First, the Judge of all the earth does right. Abraham's question in 18:25 is the bedrock of biblical faith. God does not act randomly or cruelly. He investigates before he judges. He listens to intercession. He saves the righteous even when the wicked are destroyed. You can trust his justice even when you can't understand his methods.

Second, intercession matters even when the outcome isn't what you hoped. Abraham's prayer didn't save Sodom. But it saved Lot. You may pray for something and not see the answer you wanted. That doesn't mean your prayer was wasted. God hears. God remembers. And he works in ways you may not see until much later.

Third, proximity to sin has consequences. Lot chose Sodom for its beauty and opportunity. By the time the angels arrived, the city's values had seeped into his family in ways he never intended. The people you spend time with, the environments you choose, the content you consume, these things shape you more than you think. Lot's story is a warning: don't pitch your tent toward Sodom.

Fourth, God's heroes are real people with real flaws. Abraham lied. Twice. About the same thing. And God kept working through him anyway. That isn't an excuse for dishonesty. It's a reminder that God's plan has never depended on human perfection. It depends on his faithfulness.

TALKING POINTS

1. **Abraham asked, "Will not the Judge of all the earth do right?"** Have you ever wondered whether God's actions were fair? How does Abraham's question help us think about that?

2. **God would have spared Sodom for ten righteous people.** What does that tell you about the value God places on the righteous? Can the presence of faithful people make a difference in a wicked community?

3. **Lot was dragged out of Sodom by angels. He hesitated even as the city was about to be destroyed.** Why do you think

it's so hard to leave behind something familiar, even when it's harmful?

4. **Abraham repeated the same lie about Sarah that he'd told in Egypt.** Why do you think people keep falling into the same sins? What does it take to actually break a pattern?

5. **A pagan king acted more honorably than Abraham in Genesis 20.** What does that tell us about the fact that God can use anyone, and that being "chosen" doesn't mean being morally superior to everyone else?

The fire has fallen. The cities are ash. Lot is rescued but broken. Abraham has stumbled again but remains in God's grip. And the promise still stands: within a year, Sarah will hold a baby in her arms. The longest wait of her life is almost over.

Turn the page.

8

LAUGHTER AND TEARS

In Disney's The Fox and the Hound, an old widow named Tweed finds a baby fox orphaned in the woods. She takes him in, names him Tod, and raises him as her own. She feeds him from a bottle. She lets him sleep by the fire. She talks to him, scolds him, and loves him the way you love something small and helpless that depends on you completely.

But Tod grows up. And as he does, the world outside the widow's fence gets more dangerous. Her neighbor, a hunter named Amos Slade, has a hunting dog named Copper, and Slade has sworn to destroy the fox. The longer Tod stays, the more likely it is that he'll be killed. The widow knows it. She fights against it for as long as she can. But one morning, she makes the hardest decision of her life.

She puts Tod in her truck and drives him to a game preserve deep in the forest. She opens the tailgate, sets him down, and walks away. Tod stands there, confused, watching her leave. And the camera holds on the widow's face as she drives off, tears streaming, gripping the steering wheel, having just willingly given up the thing she loved most in the world because keeping him would have destroyed him.

It's one of the most heartbreaking scenes in any Disney movie. Not because something is taken from her. Because she *chose* to let go.

Genesis 21–22 is the story of a father who received the child he'd waited a lifetime for, and then was asked to place that child on an altar. It's the most emotionally devastating passage in the entire book. And how Abraham responded on that mountain determined the shape of the rest of the Bible.

THE LAUGHTER FINALLY COMES

"Now the LORD was gracious to Sarah as he had said, and the LORD did for Sarah what he had promised." After twenty-five years of waiting. After Hagar and Ishmael. After two episodes of Abraham lying to foreign kings. After laughter born of disbelief from both Abraham and Sarah. After all of it, the promise was fulfilled.

Sarah became pregnant. She bore a son. Abraham named him Isaac, just as God had commanded. The name means "he laughs," and the laughter that had once been bitter doubt was now pure, ringing joy. Sarah said, "God has brought me laughter, and everyone who hears about this will laugh with me." She marveled at the absurdity of it: "Who would have said to Abraham that Sarah would nurse children? Yet I have borne him a son in his old age."

Abraham was one hundred years old. Sarah was ninety. And there, in their arms, was a baby boy. Living proof that nothing is too hard for the Lord. On the eighth day, Abraham circumcised Isaac as God had commanded. Every piece of the promise was clicking into place.

If this were the end of the story, it would be one of the most beautiful in all of Scripture. But Genesis has a way of following joy with heartbreak. And the shadow was already forming.

A HOUSE DIVIDED

As Isaac grew, trouble returned. During a feast celebrating Isaac's weaning, Sarah saw Ishmael, now a teenager, mocking the younger boy. Whatever Ishmael was doing, it was enough to send Sarah into a fury. She demanded that Abraham send Hagar and Ishmael away permanently: "Get rid of that slave woman and her son, for that slave woman's son will never share in the inheritance with my son Isaac."

The demand tore Abraham apart. Ishmael was his son too. He had loved Ishmael for over thirteen years before Isaac was born. The text says the matter "distressed Abraham greatly."

But God told Abraham to listen to Sarah. Not because Sarah's motives were pure, but because God's plan required it. "It is through Isaac that your offspring will be reckoned." Isaac was the child of promise, the one through whom the covenant would continue. God also reassured Abraham that Ishmael would not be abandoned: "I will make the son of the maidservant into a nation also, because he is your offspring."

Early the next morning, Abraham gave Hagar bread and a skin of water and sent her and Ishmael away. The provisions were meager for a desert journey, barely enough for a few days. When the water ran out, Hagar left Ishmael under a bush and sat down a distance away. She couldn't watch her son die. She sobbed.

But God heard the boy crying. The angel of God called from heaven: "Do not be afraid. God has heard the boy crying as he lies there. Lift the boy up and take him by the hand, for I will make him into a great nation." Then God opened Hagar's eyes, and she saw a well. Water. Life. A future.

The text adds a quiet, powerful line: "God was with the boy as he grew up." Ishmael was outside the covenant line, but he was not outside God's care. God saw him, heard him, and stayed with him. Ishmael grew into an archer in the wilderness, married an Egyptian woman, and became the father of a nation, just as God had promised.

The household was divided. One son stayed. One son left. But both were held in the hands of God.

THE TEST

Then came the moment that defines everything. "Some time later God tested Abraham."

The narrator tells us up front what's happening. This is a test, not a punishment. God is not trying to destroy Abraham. He is revealing what is in Abraham's heart. But Abraham doesn't know it's a test. All he hears is the command.

"Take your son, your only son, whom you love, Isaac, and go to the region of Moriah. Sacrifice him there as a burnt offering on a mountain I will show you."

Read those words slowly. Feel the weight of them. God didn't say "your son." He said "your son, your only son, whom you love, Isaac." Each phrase tightens the knot. Each word makes it more impossible. God was making absolutely certain that Abraham understood what was being asked.

This was Isaac. The child of the promise. The boy they had waited twenty-five years for. The one through whom all the nations of the earth were supposed to be blessed. The living proof that God keeps his word. And God was telling Abraham to kill him.

Everything was at stake. Not just a father's love for his son, although that alone would have been devastating. The entire future of the promise hung in the balance. If Isaac died, there would be no descendants. No great nation. No blessing to the nations. No covenant fulfilled. The promise itself would die on that altar.

What did Abraham do?

"Early the next morning Abraham got up and loaded his donkey."

No argument. No delay. No negotiation like he'd done at Sodom. He got up early and started walking.

THE WALK TO MORIAH

For three days, Abraham and Isaac traveled toward the mountain. Three days of walking with his son, knowing what was waiting at the top. The text says nothing about what Abraham felt during those three days. It doesn't have to. The silence says everything.

When they reached the region, Abraham told his servants, "Stay here with the donkey while I and the boy go over there. We will worship and then *we* will come back to you."

Did you catch that? "We will come back." Abraham told his servants that both of them would return. The book of Hebrews explains this: "Abraham reasoned that God could even raise the dead" (Hebrews 11:19). Abraham didn't understand how, but he believed that even if Isaac died on that mountain, God would bring him back. The promise was too sure to fail. God had said that through Isaac his offspring would be reckoned, and Abraham believed God meant it.

That's not blind obedience. That's faith so deep it looks insane from the outside.

As they climbed, Isaac spoke. "Father? The fire and wood are here, but where is the lamb for the burnt offering?"

Imagine hearing that question from the boy you're about to sacrifice. Abraham's answer is one of the most important sentences in Genesis: "God himself will provide the lamb for the burnt offering, my son."

He didn't know exactly how. But he believed it.

THE ALTAR

Abraham built an altar. He arranged the wood. He bound his son and laid him on top. He reached out his hand and took the knife.

The narrative slows to a crawl. Every verb is deliberate. Built. Arranged. Bound. Laid. Reached. Took. You can feel the unbearable weight of each action. The boy who had been promised, waited for, laughed over, named, circumcised, weaned, and celebrated was now lying on a pile of wood with his father's hand on the knife.

Then the angel of the Lord called from heaven. "Abraham! Abraham!"

"Here I am."

"Do not lay a hand on the boy. Do not do anything to him. Now I know that you fear God, because you have not withheld from me your son, your only son."

Abraham looked up and saw a ram caught in a thicket by its horns. He sacrificed the ram instead of his son. And he named that place "The LORD Will Provide," a name that became a saying in Israel: "On the mountain of the LORD it will be provided."

God had provided a substitute. A life in place of a life. An offering in place of the beloved son. And on that same mountain range, centuries later, God would provide the ultimate substitute, his own Son, "the Lamb of God, who takes away the sin of the world" (John 1:29).

Then the angel spoke a second time, and for the first time in Scripture, God swore an oath by himself: "Because you have done this and have not withheld your son, your only son, I will surely bless you and make your descendants as numerous as the stars in the sky and as the sand on the seashore. Your descendants will take possession of the cities of their enemies, and through your offspring all nations on earth will be blessed, because you have obeyed me."

The test was over. Abraham had passed. And the promise was now sealed with the strongest guarantee in the universe: the oath of God.

Abraham and Isaac walked back down the mountain together. The text says they returned to the servants and went back to Beersheba. Father and son. Alive. Together.

WHAT THIS MEANS FOR US

First, God keeps his promises, but rarely on our schedule. Abraham waited twenty-five years for Isaac. If you are waiting on God for something, remember that "the appointed time" is real, even if it hasn't arrived yet. God's delays are not God's denials.

Second, the greatest test of faith is whether you'll give back what God gave you. Everything Abraham had, including Isaac, came from God. The test at Moriah wasn't whether Abraham loved his son. Of course he did. The test was whether he loved God more. At some point, every person who follows God will face a version of this question: is there anything you value more than him?

Third, God provides. "The LORD Will Provide" became the defining statement of Abraham's life. He had doubted it in Egypt. He had fumbled it with Hagar. But on Moriah, he finally, fully believed it. And God came through. Whatever mountain you're climbing right now, that truth hasn't changed.

Fourth, this story points to Jesus. A father takes his only, beloved son to a mountain to be sacrificed. The son carries the wood on his back. A substitute is provided at the last moment. The echoes of the gospel are everywhere in Genesis 22. But when it came time for God to sacrifice *his* only Son on a hill outside Jerusalem, there was no angel to stop it and no ram caught in the thicket. Jesus was the substitute. And through that sacrifice, the promise to Abraham was finally, fully, and forever kept: all nations on earth are blessed through his offspring.

TALKING POINTS

1. **Sarah said, "God has brought me laughter."** Have you ever experienced a moment where something you'd been

hoping for finally happened? How did it change the way you thought about God?

2. **Abraham was asked to give up the thing he loved most.** What would be the hardest thing for you to surrender to God? Why do you think God sometimes asks us to let go of what we value most?

3. **Abraham told Isaac, "God himself will provide." He didn't know how. He just trusted.** What does it look like to trust God when you can't see the answer yet?

4. **On the mountain of Moriah, God provided a ram as a substitute for Isaac.** How does this point to what God did for us through Jesus? What does it mean that Jesus is called "the Lamb of God"?

5. **After Moriah, the Bible never records another failure of Abraham's faith.** What do you think changed in him on that mountain? Can a single moment of obedience change the direction of your life?

The test is over. The oath is sworn. Isaac is alive, and the promise is more certain than ever. But Sarah's days are numbered, and a new generation is about to step into the story. Abraham's journey of faith is nearing its end. But the story he started is just getting started.

Turn the page.

9

ENDINGS AND BEGINNINGS

In Louisa May Alcott's *Little Women*, the March family navigates growing up, growing apart, and growing through loss. The four sisters—Meg, Jo, Beth, and Amy—begin the novel as children, full of energy and dreams, crowded together in their little house. But the story doesn't stay there. The girls grow up. They fall in love. They make choices that pull them in different directions. And then Beth gets sick.

Beth's death is the quiet heart of the novel. She doesn't die dramatically. She fades. And the family gathers around her, holds her, and lets her go. Jo, the sister who fights everything, who refuses to accept that things have to change, sits beside Beth's empty chair afterward and realizes that the family she grew up in is gone. Not destroyed. Transformed. The old season is over, and a new one is beginning, whether she's ready for it or not.

But here's the thing about *Little Women*: the ending isn't really an ending. Meg has children. Jo finds her calling. Amy finds love. The next generation is already taking shape even as the old one passes away. The story doesn't stop. It continues through the people who come after.

Genesis 23–25 is the Bible's version of that transition. The founding generation of God's covenant family is passing from the stage. Sarah dies. Abraham buries her, finds a wife for Isaac, and then dies himself. Even Ishmael's story reaches its conclusion. But woven through every funeral and farewell is evidence that the promise hasn't died with its original recipients. It's being handed to the next generation. The story goes on.

THE DEATH OF SARAH

Sarah lived 127 years, the only woman in the Bible whose exact age at death is recorded. She died at Kiriath-arba, later known as Hebron, and Abraham "went to mourn for Sarah and to weep over her."

That simple sentence carries the weight of decades. This was the woman who had followed Abraham out of Ur when God called. She had lived in tents across Canaan. She had endured famine, foreign kings, barrenness, the Hagar disaster, and years of waiting. She had laughed in disbelief when God promised a son, and then laughed with joy when Isaac was born. She had been Abraham's companion through every twist of this extraordinary story. And now she was gone.

But what Abraham did next was as much an act of faith as anything he'd done at Moriah.

He needed a place to bury her. In the ancient world, custom demanded that the dead be buried in their ancestral homeland. Abraham could have sent Sarah's body back to Mesopotamia. That would have been the expected thing. Instead, he chose to bury her in Canaan, the land God had promised to his descendants. By putting Sarah in Canaan's soil, Abraham was planting a flag. He was saying, "This is our home now. Not because we own it yet. But because God said it would be ours."

The negotiation that followed reads like an ancient real estate transaction, and it was. Abraham approached the local Hittites and asked to purchase a burial site. They offered to let him use any of their tombs for free. But Abraham didn't want a borrowed grave. He wanted to *own* the land. He insisted on buying the cave of Machpelah from a man named Ephron.

Ephron named his price: four hundred shekels of silver. It was an outrageous sum. A laborer at that time earned about ten shekels a year, so Abraham was paying roughly forty years' wages for a field and a cave. David would later buy a threshing floor for fifty shekels. Jeremiah bought a field for seventeen. Abraham didn't flinch. He weighed out the silver in full, in front of witnesses, and the deal was done.

This cave became the first and only piece of land Abraham ever legally owned in Canaan. After all the promises of property, after decades of wandering, the only ground with his name on it was a cemetery. But that cemetery was a declaration of faith. Abraham was saying to God, "I believe you will give this land to my children, even though I will not live to see it."

He buried Sarah there. And years later, Abraham himself would be buried in the same cave, alongside the wife who had shared his impossible journey.

A BRIDE FOR ISAAC

With Sarah gone and Abraham growing old, one critical piece of the promise remained unfulfilled: Isaac needed a wife. Without a wife, there would be no children. Without children, the promise of descendants as numerous as the stars would die in a single generation.

Abraham summoned his most trusted servant, likely the chief steward of his household, and gave him a mission. Go back to my family's homeland in Mesopotamia and find a wife for Isaac from among my relatives. Two things were non-negotiable. First, Isaac must not marry a Canaanite woman. Abraham had seen the corruption of Canaan up close and didn't want it woven into the family's future. Second, Isaac must not go back to Mesopotamia himself. God had called Abraham *out* of that land. Going back would be a step in the wrong direction.

The servant traveled over five hundred miles with ten camels loaded with gifts. When he arrived at the town of Nahor, he stopped at the well and prayed one of the most specific prayers in all of Scripture. He asked God for a sign: let the woman you've chosen be the one who offers water not just to me but to my camels too. Watering ten camels after a long journey would require hauling hundreds of gallons of water. It would take strength, generosity, and a willingness to serve a complete stranger.

Before the servant even finished praying, a young woman named Rebekah arrived at the well. She was beautiful. She was from Abraham's extended family, the granddaughter of Abraham's brother Nahor. And she did exactly what the servant had prayed for. She drew water for him and then said, "I'll draw water for your camels too, until they have had enough to drink." She ran back and forth to the well until every camel was satisfied.

The servant stood and watched, "without saying a word, to learn whether or not the LORD had made his journey successful." When she finished, he gave her gold jewelry and asked whose family she belonged to. When he learned she was from Nahor's line, he bowed and worshiped God on the spot.

The servant told Rebekah's family the whole story. Laban, her brother, and Bethuel, her father, responded, "This is from the LORD; we can say nothing to you one way or the other." They asked Rebekah directly: "Will you go with this man?" Her answer was immediate: "I will go."

Think about what she was agreeing to. She had never met Isaac. She had never seen Canaan. She was leaving her family, her home, and everything familiar to marry a man she'd only heard about from a servant who showed up at her well. She was doing what Abraham had done a generation earlier: leaving everything behind on the strength of a promise.

When Rebekah arrived in Canaan, Isaac was out in a field. He looked up and saw the camels approaching. Rebekah looked up and saw him. She dismounted, covered herself with a veil, and the servant told Isaac everything that had happened. Isaac brought her into his mother Sarah's tent and married her. The text adds a quiet, tender note: "So she became his wife, and he loved her; and Isaac was comforted after his mother's death."

The promise had a future again.

THE DEATH OF ABRAHAM

Abraham lived 175 years. After Sarah's death, he married a woman named Keturah and had six more sons through her. But Isaac remained the sole heir of the covenant. Abraham gave gifts to his other sons and sent them away to the east, ensuring that Isaac's inheritance was secure.

When Abraham died, the text says he was "gathered to his people," a phrase that implies not just death but reunion, an existence beyond the grave where the dead are not alone. He was buried in the cave of Machpelah, next to Sarah. And the ones who buried him were Isaac and Ishmael, together.

That detail is easy to miss, but it's remarkable. The two brothers, the one who stayed and the one who was sent away, stood side by side at their father's grave. Whatever tensions had driven them apart, they came together to honor the man who had loved them both. It's a brief, quiet moment of reconciliation in a story full of family conflict.

After Abraham's death, "God blessed his son Isaac." The torch had been passed. The promise continued.

THE LINE OF ISHMAEL

Genesis 25:12–18 gives us the genealogy of Ishmael. He fathered twelve sons, who became twelve tribal rulers, fulfilling God's promise to Hagar and Abraham that Ishmael would become a great nation. Ishmael lived 137 years and died. His descendants settled in the region stretching from Egypt toward Assyria.

This genealogy is brief, but its placement is deliberate. Genesis has a pattern: whenever the narrative is about to narrow its focus to the chosen line, it first closes the book on the other branch. It did this with Cain before focusing on Seth. It did this with Japheth and Ham before focusing on Shem. Now it closes Ishmael's story before turning to Isaac and his sons.

But notice: God kept every promise he made about Ishmael. Twelve sons. A great nation. The blessing was real. God's faithfulness extended to both of Abraham's sons, even though only one carried the covenant forward.

WHAT THIS MEANS FOR US

First, faith speaks loudest in the ordinary moments. Abraham's most dramatic act of faith was the binding of Isaac. But his quietest might have been buying a cemetery. There was no angel, no voice from heaven, just an old man paying too much for a cave because he believed God's promise about the land. Some of the most important acts of faith in your life won't feel dramatic. They'll feel ordinary. A decision to stay faithful. A choice to keep trusting. A willingness to invest in a future you may never see.

Second, God works through the choices of ordinary people. The servant prayed at a well. Rebekah chose to water the camels. Laban opened his home. Each decision was human, but God was weaving them all together into something none of them could have orchestrated on their own. You don't have to see the whole picture to play your part in it. Just be faithful with the moment in front of you.

Third, endings are not the end. Sarah died. Abraham died. Ishmael's story closed. But the promise didn't die with any of them. It passed to Isaac, to Rebekah, and eventually to their sons. When someone you love is gone, or when a season of life comes to an end, it can feel like the story is over. It's not. God writes across generations. The chapter changes. The story continues.

Fourth, God keeps his promises to everyone he makes them to. Ishmael received exactly what God had promised: twelve sons, a great nation, a future. He wasn't the child of the covenant, but he was never forgotten. If God has made you a promise, even one that seems smaller than what he promised someone else, he will keep it.

TALKING POINTS

1. **Abraham paid an outrageous price for a cave in Canaan to bury Sarah.** Why was this act of faith so significant? What was he saying about God's promises by buying that land?

2. **The servant prayed for a very specific sign at the well, and God answered before the prayer was even finished.** What does this tell you about how God guides his people? Have you ever experienced God's guidance in an unexpected way?

3. **Rebekah said "I will go" without ever having met Isaac.** What kind of courage does that take? How is her decision similar to Abraham's original call to leave his homeland?

4. **Isaac and Ishmael buried their father together.** What does that small detail suggest about their relationship? Can family divisions ever be healed?

5. **Genesis closes the stories of Sarah, Abraham, and Ishmael in these chapters before moving on to Isaac.** Why do you think endings matter in God's story? How does knowing that God works across generations change the way you think about your own life?

The founding generation is gone. Sarah rests in the cave at Machpelah. Abraham lies beside her. Ishmael's line stretches into the desert. And Isaac, the child of laughter, the boy who was bound on Moriah and given back, now carries the promise forward with a wife named Rebekah.

But Rebekah, like Sarah before her, is barren. And the struggle over who will carry the promise next is about to tear another family apart.

Turn the page.

10

THE DECEIVER AND THE BLESSING

In the movie *Aladdin*, a street thief named Aladdin wants desperately to be something more than what he is. He's poor, hungry, and invisible to the people who matter. When he stumbles onto a magic lamp and meets a genie, Aladdin sees his chance. He wishes to become a prince, someone worthy of Princess Jasmine and the life he's always dreamed about. The genie transforms him. He rides into the city on a parade of elephants. He wears silk and gold. Everyone bows.

But it's a lie. Underneath the costume, Aladdin is still a street rat. And the longer he pretends to be someone he isn't, the more tangled the deception becomes. He lies to Jasmine. He lies to the sultan. He almost loses the genie, the girl, and his own life because he's too afraid to let people see who he really is. It's only at the end, when the disguise is stripped away and Aladdin stands exposed for who he actually is, that the real story begins. Jasmine chooses the real Aladdin, not the fake prince. And the truth turns out to be better than the lie ever was.

Genesis 25–28 introduces us to a man whose entire identity was built on deception. His name was Jacob. He schemed his way into a birthright, cheated his way into a blessing, and ran for his life when it all fell apart. But in the middle of his escape, alone in the dark with a stone for a pillow, God showed up. And what God offered Jacob was something no amount of trickery could ever obtain.

TWO NATIONS IN ONE WOMB

Barrenness ran in the family. Sarah had been barren. Now Rebekah was too. But Isaac responded differently than his father had. He didn't devise a plan. He didn't take a second wife. He prayed. For twenty years, Isaac pleaded with God on behalf of his wife. And God answered. Rebekah conceived.

But the pregnancy was brutal. The twins inside her weren't just kicking. They were crushing each other. The pain was so intense that Rebekah cried out to God, "Why is this happening to me?" God's answer was a prophecy:

"Two nations are in your womb, and two peoples from within you will be separated; one people will be stronger than the other, and the older will serve the younger."

That last line shattered the convention of the ancient world. The firstborn always received the greater inheritance, the leadership of the family, the lion's share of everything. God was announcing, before the boys were even born, that he would reverse the natural order. His choice wouldn't be based on birth order or merit. It would be based on his own sovereign will.

The twins were born as different as two brothers could be. Esau came out red and hairy, a rough-and-tumble outdoorsman who loved hunting and the open field. Jacob came out gripping his brother's heel, and the name stuck: Jacob, "heel-grabber," which also carried the sense of "deceiver." Esau became Isaac's favorite. Jacob was Rebekah's. The favoritism would poison everything.

A BIRTHRIGHT FOR A BOWL OF SOUP

One day Esau came in from hunting, exhausted and starving. Jacob was cooking stew. Esau demanded some, and Jacob saw his opening. "First sell me your birthright," he said.

The birthright was the firstborn's right to a double share of the family inheritance and leadership of the household. It was sacred. It represented the future of the entire family line. And Esau traded it for a bowl of soup.

"What good is the birthright to me?" Esau said. He swore an oath, handed over his future, ate the stew, and walked away. The narrator's verdict is blunt: "So Esau despised his birthright." In a book where explicit moral commentary is rare, that sentence is a thunderclap. Esau didn't just make a bad trade. He treated something holy as worthless. The New Testament uses him as a warning: don't sacrifice an eternal blessing for a temporary craving (Hebrews 12:16).

But Jacob wasn't innocent either. He exploited his brother's weakness for personal gain. The man who would carry the covenant forward got his start through manipulation, not faith. That tension runs through the next several chapters and won't be resolved until Jacob learns, the hard way, that God doesn't need a con artist to accomplish his plans.

THE STOLEN BLESSING

Years later, Isaac was old and nearly blind. Believing he might die soon, he called Esau and asked him to hunt some game and prepare a special meal. After the meal, Isaac would give Esau the patriarchal blessing, the formal pronouncement that transferred leadership, authority, and God's favor to the next generation. Once spoken, a blessing of this kind could not be taken back. It had a life of its own.

But Rebekah overheard. And she hatched a plan. She told Jacob to bring two goats from the flock. She cooked them to taste like wild game. She dressed Jacob in Esau's clothes so he would smell like his brother. She covered his smooth hands and neck with goatskins so he would feel hairy to his blind father's touch. Then she sent Jacob in to steal the blessing.

Isaac was suspicious. "The voice is the voice of Jacob, but the hands are the hands of Esau," he said. But his other senses—the rough skin, the smell of the field—convinced him. He blessed Jacob with fertility, abundance, and dominion: "May nations serve you and peoples bow down to you. Be lord over your brothers."

The moment Jacob left, Esau walked in with the real meal. The truth hit Isaac like a shockwave. He "trembled violently" when he realized what had happened. Esau's reaction was devastating: "He burst out with a loud and bitter cry." He begged for a blessing of his own, but the primary blessing was gone, transferred irrevocably to Jacob.

Esau's grief turned to rage. He resolved to kill his brother the moment their father died. When Rebekah heard about the death threat, she told Jacob to flee to her brother Laban in Haran until Esau's fury cooled down.

Everyone in this story is guilty of something. Isaac tried to bless Esau despite knowing God's prophecy that the older would serve the younger. Rebekah engineered a deception instead of trusting God to work it out. Jacob lied to his blind father's face, even invoking God's name to sell the con: "The LORD your God gave me success." Esau had already sold his birthright and had married Canaanite women against his parents' wishes. There is no hero in Genesis 27. Only broken people and a God who somehow works through the mess they make.

A STONE FOR A PILLOW

Jacob fled. The homebody who had always stayed near the tents was now alone on a five-hundred-mile journey to a place he'd never been, running from a brother who wanted him dead. He had the blessing, but he had lost his family, his home, and his safety. The deceiver had gotten everything he schemed for, and it had cost him everything he had.

On the first or second night, somewhere between Beersheba and Haran, Jacob stopped because the sun had set. He grabbed a stone, put it under his head, and fell asleep.

And then God spoke to him for the first time. In a dream, Jacob saw a stairway stretching from earth to heaven. Angels were ascending and descending on it, going out on God's errands and returning. And there at the top stood the LORD himself, who said:

"I am the LORD, the God of your father Abraham and the God of Isaac. I will give you and your descendants the land on which you are lying. Your descendants will be like the dust of the earth, and you will spread out to the west and to the east, to the north and to the south. All peoples on earth will be blessed through you and your offspring. I am with you and will watch over you wherever you go, and I will bring you back to this land. I will not leave you until I have done what I have promised you."

Stop and think about the timing. Jacob had just lied to his father, stolen a blessing, and fled for his life. He had done nothing to deserve God's attention, let alone God's promises. And yet here was God, standing at the top of a stairway, voluntarily binding himself to a cheater and a runaway. Every promise God had made to Abraham and Isaac—land, descendants, blessing for the nations—was now extended to Jacob. Not because Jacob had earned it. Because God had chosen it.

Jacob woke up terrified. "Surely the LORD is in this place, and I was not aware of it," he said. "How awesome is this place! This is none other than the house of God; this is the gate of heaven." He set up the stone as a pillar, poured oil on it, and named the place Bethel, meaning "house of God." The old name of the place had been Lu/ The name change was fitting. Something was beginning to shift.

Jacob made a vow: if God would be with him, protect him, and bring him home, then the Lord would be his God. It wasn't the most mature prayer ever prayed. It sounds more like a bargain than a surrender. But it was a start. For the first time in the narrative, Jacob was talking to God instead of scheming around him.

Centuries later, Jesus pointed back to this moment. He told his disciple Nathanael, "You will see heaven opened, and the angels of God ascending and descending on the Son of Man" (John 1:51). Jesus himself was the true stairway between heaven and earth. The connection Jacob glimpsed in a dream, Jesus made permanent through the cross.

WHAT THIS MEANS FOR US

First, God's choice is based on grace, not performance. Jacob didn't earn the blessing. He stole it. And yet God chose him anyway. That pattern runs through the entire Bible: God doesn't choose the most qualified. He chooses the most unlikely, and then transforms them into something extraordinary. If you feel unworthy of God's attention, you're in good company. So was Jacob.

Second, manipulation always costs more than it gains. Jacob got the birthright and the blessing, but he lost his home, his family, and his safety. Rebekah never saw her favorite son again. Scheming may produce short-term results, but it always extracts a long-term price. God doesn't need your help to keep his promises. He needs your trust.

Third, God meets us in our lowest moments. Jacob was alone, afraid, and on the run when God appeared to him. He wasn't in a temple. He wasn't praying. He was sleeping on a rock. God doesn't wait for us to get our lives together before he shows up. He comes to us in the dark, on the worst night, with promises we don't deserve.

Fourth, the real blessing can't be stolen. Jacob tried to grab the blessing through deception, and it worked on a human level. But the real blessing, God's covenant presence and promise, was given freely at Bethel, no tricks required. The things that matter most in life can't be obtained by scheming. They come from God, on his terms, as gifts of grace.

TALKING POINTS

1. **God told Rebekah before the twins were born that "the older will serve the younger."** Why do you think Rebekah still felt the need to help God's plan along through deception? Have you ever tried to "help" God when you should have just trusted him?

2. **Esau traded his birthright for a bowl of soup.** What are some things people today trade their future for because of short-term desires? How do you avoid making that mistake?

3. **There's no hero in Genesis 27. Everyone is guilty of something.** What does it tell you about God that he can work through deeply flawed people? Does that excuse their behavior?

4. **God appeared to Jacob at his lowest point, not his highest.** Why do you think God chose that moment? Have you ever experienced God's presence when you least expected it?

5. **Jesus said he was the true stairway between heaven and earth (John 1:51).** What does it mean that the connection Jacob saw in a dream became a permanent reality through Jesus?

Jacob is heading east with nothing but a promise and a stone pillar behind him. Ahead of him lies his uncle Laban, a man who will teach him what it feels like to be on the receiving end of deception. And somewhere in those hard years, the deceiver will begin to change.

Turn the page.

11

THE DECEIVER DECEIVED

In Charlotte Brontë's *Jane Eyre*, a young governess named Jane falls deeply in love with her employer, Mr. Rochester. He's brilliant and passionate, and he loves her back. They plan to marry. But on the morning of the wedding, Jane discovers that Rochester has been hiding a terrible secret: he is already married. His first wife, mentally ill and dangerous, has been locked away in the attic of his own house for years. Everything Rochester told Jane was shaded by this lie. The love was real, but the deception poisoned it.

Jane is devastated. She loves Rochester, but she will not build her future on a lie. She walks away. And what follows is a long, painful season of exile and hardship. Jane wanders alone, nearly starves, and has to rebuild her life from nothing. It takes years. But in that exile, she discovers who she is apart from Rochester. She comes into her own inheritance, finds her own identity, and eventually returns to Rochester, but only after he has been humbled, broken, and changed by the consequences of his deception.

It's a story about what happens when you meet someone who lies as well as you do. And it's a story about how exile, suffering, and time can transform a person into someone better than they were before.

Genesis 29–31 tells a similar story. Jacob, the deceiver, arrives at his uncle Laban's home and meets his match. For twenty years, two con artists circle each other, each trying to come out on top. But woven through the scheming and the heartbreak is the quiet, relentless work of God, building a family, keeping his promises, and slowly reshaping a liar into a patriarch.

LOVE AT FIRST SIGHT

Jacob arrived in Haran with nothing. When Abraham's servant had made this same journey a generation earlier, he came with ten camels loaded with gifts and a prayer on his lips. Jacob came empty-handed and, as far as the text tells us, without a prayer.

At a well outside the city, Jacob met shepherds who knew his uncle Laban. While they were talking, Laban's younger daughter Rachel arrived with her father's sheep. The text says Rachel was "lovely in form and beautiful." Jacob took one look at her, rolled the heavy stone off the well's mouth by himself, watered her flock, kissed her, and wept out loud.

It was instant, overwhelming love. And it would cost him everything.

After staying a month, Jacob struck a deal with Laban. He would work seven years in exchange for Rachel's hand in marriage. The average bride price at the time was about thirty or forty shekels of silver, roughly three or four years' wages. Laban was charging nearly double. But Jacob was broke and lovesick, and the text says the seven years "seemed like only a few days to him because of his love for her."

When the seven years were up, Laban threw a wedding feast. The celebration involved heavy drinking, as was the custom. And when morning came, Jacob discovered the unthinkable.

It wasn't Rachel in the marriage bed. It was Leah, her older sister.

The deceiver had been deceived.

THE WRONG WIFE

Jacob was furious. "What is this you have done to me?" he demanded. "I served you for Rachel, didn't I? Why have you deceived me?" Laban's excuse was thin: "It is not our custom here to give the younger daughter in marriage before the older one." If that was the rule, why hadn't he mentioned it seven years earlier?

The irony is devastating and intentional. Jacob, who had dressed in his brother's clothes and pretended to be the first-born to steal a blessing, was now on the receiving end of a scheme involving the wrong sibling. He had exploited his father's blindness; now the darkness of the wedding tent had exploited his. The man who had cheated the older brother out of his rights was told that the older sister must come first. As the apostle Paul would later write, "A man reaps what he sows" (Galatians 6:7).

Laban offered a deal: finish the wedding week with Leah, and then you can marry Rachel too, but you'll owe another seven years of labor. Jacob agreed. He married Rachel a week later. And the damage was done.

The text says it plainly: Jacob loved Rachel more than Leah. The word used for Leah's status can mean "hated" or "unloved." Leah was not the wife Jacob wanted. She knew it. Everyone knew it. And the children she would bear would carry the weight of that rejection in their very names.

But here is where Genesis does something remarkable. Caught in the crossfire of this toxic marriage, Leah becomes the quiet hero of the story. Not Jacob. Not Rachel. Leah.

A BABY WAR

"When the LORD saw that Leah was not loved, he opened her womb, but Rachel was barren." God saw the unloved wife and acted on her behalf, just as he had seen Hagar in the desert. Rachel had Jacob's heart. Leah had God's attention.

Leah's first four sons were named as prayers and cries to God. Reuben: "The LORD has seen my misery. Surely my husband will love me now." Simeon: "Because the LORD heard that I am not loved, he gave me this one too." Levi: "Now at last my husband will become attached to me." Judah: "This time I will praise the LORD." Each name was a window into a woman's heartbreak, and each one was a testament to her faith. Even in her pain, Leah kept turning to God.

Rachel, meanwhile, was consumed by jealousy. She demanded of Jacob, "Give me children, or I'll die!" Jacob's response was sharp: "Am I in the place of God? He's the one who has kept you from having children." Unlike his father Isaac, who had prayed for Rebekah's barrenness for twenty years, Jacob didn't intercede. He snapped.

What followed was a rivalry that reads like a competition,

painful and exhausting. Rachel gave her servant Bilhah to Jacob as a surrogate, producing Dan and Naphtali. Leah countered by giving her servant Zilpah, producing Gad and Asher. Then came the mandrake incident, where Leah's son Reuben found plants believed to be a fertility cure in the ancient world. Rachel traded a night with Jacob in exchange for the mandrakes. In a bitter twist, Leah conceived again that very night. She went on to bear two more sons, Issachar and Zebulun, and a daughter, Dinah. Rachel's mandrakes did nothing.

Finally, "God remembered Rachel." He opened her womb, and she bore Joseph, a name that expressed both gratitude for the end of her shame and hope for another son.

Through all the scheming, jealousy, and heartbreak, God was building the twelve tribes of Israel. The family was a mess. The marriages were broken. The motives were mixed. And yet, out of this dysfunction, God was assembling the people through whom the Messiah would eventually come. Judah, Leah's fourth son, the one whose name meant "praise," would be the ancestor of King David and ultimately of Jesus Christ. The unloved wife gave birth to the line of the Savior.

God's purposes don't require perfect families. They require a faithful God.

THE GREAT ESCAPE

After Rachel bore Joseph, Jacob told Laban he wanted to go home. He had now worked fourteen years for his two wives. But Laban wasn't ready to let him go. He admitted openly that he'd been blessed by God because of Jacob's presence and wanted to keep the arrangement going.

They struck a new deal. Jacob would continue working for Laban, and his wages would be every speckled, spotted, or dark-colored animal born in the flocks. These were normally a small minority, so Laban thought he was getting the better end of the bargain. He even cheated by removing all the currently spotted animals and putting a three-day distance between them and Jacob's flocks, making it nearly impossible for Jacob to build a herd.

But God had other plans. Over the next six years, Jacob's flocks multiplied dramatically. The text credits God, not Jacob's methods, as the source of his prosperity. Jacob grew enormously wealthy in livestock, servants, camels, and donkeys. Laban's sons noticed, and the family's attitude toward Jacob turned hostile. "Jacob has taken everything our father owned," they grumbled.

Then God spoke to Jacob directly: "Go back to the land of your fathers and to your relatives, and I will be with you."

Jacob called Rachel and Leah to the fields for a private meeting. For once, the two rival wives agreed on something. "Do we still have any share in the inheritance of our father's estate?" they asked. "He has used up what was paid for us. Surely all the wealth that God took away from our father belongs to us and our children. So do whatever God has told you." Laban had cheated even his own daughters out of their rightful inheritance. They were done with him.

While Laban was away shearing sheep, Jacob packed up everything and fled. Three days later, Laban found out and gave chase. He caught up after seven days. The confrontation could have been violent, but God appeared to Laban in a dream the night before and warned him: "Be careful not to say anything to Jacob, either good or bad."

What followed was a tense exchange. Laban accused Jacob of sneaking away like a thief. Jacob fired back with twenty years of pent-up grievance: "I worked fourteen years for your two daughters and six years for your flocks, and you changed my wages ten times. If the God of my father had not been with me, you would surely have sent me away empty-handed." Behind Jacob's anger was a growing conviction. God had been with him. God had protected him. God had prospered him despite Laban's relentless cheating.

They made a treaty. They piled up stones as a boundary marker and agreed never to cross it with hostile intent. Laban invoked his gods, Jacob invoked the God of his father Isaac. Then Laban kissed his grandchildren, blessed his daughters, and went home.

Two decades in Haran were over. Jacob had arrived with nothing and was leaving with two wives, two servants, eleven sons, a daughter, and enormous wealth. More importantly, he was leaving with something he hadn't brought with him: a growing awareness that God, not his own cleverness, was the author of his story.

WHAT THIS MEANS FOR US

First, you reap what you sow. Jacob deceived his father and cheated his brother. In Haran, he was deceived by Laban and cheated at every turn. That's not coincidence. That's the principle of sowing and reaping at work. The way you treat people has a way of coming back to you.

Second, God sees the overlooked. Leah was unloved and overlooked. But God opened her womb, gave her children, and placed in her line the ancestry of Jesus himself. If you have ever felt like the second choice, the one nobody picks first, Leah's story says you are not invisible to God. He sees. He acts. And he may be doing something through you that nobody else can see yet.

Third, God uses broken situations for his purposes. This family was a disaster. Deception, rivalry, jealousy, favoritism, surrogate schemes, and twenty years of exploitation by Laban. And yet, out of this wreckage, God built the twelve tribes of Israel. Your family doesn't have to be perfect for God to work through it. His purposes don't depend on your circumstances. They depend on his faithfulness.

Fourth, God keeps his Bethel promise. At Bethel, God had told Jacob, "I am with you and will watch over you wherever you go, and I will bring you back to this land." Twenty years later, that's exactly what happened. God's promises don't expire, even when the journey is longer and harder than you ever expected.

TALKING POINTS

1. **Jacob was deceived by Laban in the same way he had deceived his father.** Have you ever experienced the consequences of treating someone badly? What did it teach you?

2. **Leah was unloved by Jacob, but God saw her and blessed her.** Why do you think God pays special attention to people who are overlooked or rejected? How does that change the way you treat people?

3. **Rachel and Leah both had something the other wanted. Rachel had Jacob's love; Leah had children.** Why is it so easy to focus on what we don't have instead of what we do? How does gratitude help?

4. **Jacob acknowledged that God, not his own cleverness, was the source of his prosperity.** Why is it important to recognize that our blessings come from God? What happens when we forget?

5. **God told Jacob to go home, and even Laban's own daughters agreed it was time to leave.** Have you ever sensed God leading you to make a big change? How did you know it was the right time?

Jacob has left Haran behind. Laban is gone. But the road ahead leads straight toward the one person Jacob fears most in the world: his brother Esau. Twenty years ago, Esau swore to kill him. And now Jacob is walking right back into his path.

Turn the page.

12

WRESTLING WITH GOD

In the movie *Brave*, a Scottish princess named Merida is determined to control her own destiny. Her mother, Queen Elinor, insists she follow tradition and accept an arranged marriage. Merida refuses. She fights. She argues. She enters an archery contest and humiliates the suitors in front of the entire kingdom. And when none of that works, she buys a spell from a witch to "change her fate."

The spell turns her mother into a bear.

Suddenly, the woman Merida has been fighting against is helpless, unable to speak, hunted by her own husband who doesn't recognize her. Everything Merida grabbed for — freedom, independence, control — has backfired catastrophically. The person she loves most in the world is paying the price for Merida's stubbornness.

The breakthrough doesn't come through another act of strength. It comes when Merida finally breaks. She stops fighting. She kneels beside her mother, weeps, and says the words she's been too proud to say: "This is all my fault. I did this to you." She mends the tapestry she had torn in anger, a symbol of the relationship she'd ripped apart. And in that moment of honesty and humility, the spell is broken. The mother is restored. And Merida walks forward as a different person—not because she got stronger, but because she finally stopped pretending she didn't need anyone.

Genesis 32–36 is the story of a man who spent his entire life trying to stay in control. He grabbed, schemed, and manipulated his way through every crisis. But on the banks of a river, in the middle of the night, God took hold of him and wouldn't let go. By sunrise, Jacob was limping. And for the first time in his life, he was walking in the right direction.

THE NIGHT AT THE JABBOK

Jacob was heading home, and he was terrified. Twenty years had passed since he'd stolen Esau's blessing and fled for his life. Now he was walking straight toward the brother who had sworn to kill him. When his scouts reported that Esau was coming with four hundred men, the number of a small army, Jacob "was in great fear and distress."

He did two things. First, he schemed. He divided his family and flocks into two groups, reasoning that if Esau attacked one, the other might escape. He sent ahead an enormous gift of over five hundred animals, arranged in waves designed to overwhelm his brother with generosity before the two of them came face to face.

But then Jacob did something he had rarely done before. He prayed. And it was the most honest prayer of his life. He reminded God of his promises. He admitted that he didn't deserve any of the kindness God had shown him. "I am not worthy of all the unfailing love and faithfulness you have shown to me," he said. "I was afraid. Save me, please."

It was a real prayer from a desperate man. But even in that prayer, Jacob still didn't call God "my God." That was about to change.

That night, after sending his family across the Jabbok River, Jacob was alone. And a man appeared and wrestled with him until daybreak.

The identity of this mysterious figure is one of the most debated questions in Genesis. The text calls him "a man." Jacob later said he had seen God face to face. The prophet Hosea called the figure an angel. Whoever he was, the encounter was physical, exhausting, and transformative.

They wrestled all night. Jacob, the lifelong grabber, held on with everything he had. When the figure saw that he could not overpower Jacob, he touched Jacob's hip socket and wrenched it out of joint. Even then, Jacob wouldn't let go. "I will not let you go unless you bless me," he gasped.

The figure asked a devastating question: "What is your name?"

It wasn't a request for information. It was a demand for confession. The last time someone had asked Jacob his name in a pivotal moment, he had lied: "I am Esau" (27:19). This time, there was nowhere to hide. "Jacob," he said. The Deceiver. The Grabber. That's who I am.

"Your name will no longer be Jacob, but Israel," the figure said, "because you have struggled with God and with humans and have overcome."

Jacob asked for the figure's name in return. He didn't get it. But he received a blessing. And when the sun rose, Jacob walked away from the Jabbok with a new name and a permanent limp. Every step for the rest of his life would remind him of the night God broke him open.

He named the place Peniel, meaning "face of God," because, he said, "I saw God face to face, and yet my life was spared."

THE REUNION

The next morning, Jacob looked up and saw Esau approaching with his four hundred men. He arranged his family behind him, with the servants and their children in front, Leah and her children next, and Rachel and Joseph last, the most protected position. Then Jacob walked out ahead of them all and bowed to the ground seven times as he approached his brother.

What happened next is one of the most surprising moments in Genesis.

Esau ran to Jacob, threw his arms around him, and wept. No violence. No revenge. No reckoning. Just a brother's embrace.

Jacob had spent days preparing for war. God gave him reconciliation instead. When Jacob tried to explain the lavish gifts he'd sent ahead, Esau said, "I already have plenty, my brother. Keep what you have for yourself." Jacob insisted: "Please accept my present, because seeing your face is like seeing the face of God, and you have received me so graciously."

That phrase is extraordinary. Jacob had seen the face of God at Peniel the night before. Now he saw God's mercy reflected in his brother's forgiveness. The man he feared most in the world turned out to be the instrument of grace he needed most.

Esau offered to travel together, but Jacob declined, citing the slow pace of his children and livestock. He promised to follow Esau to his home in Seir but instead settled at Succoth and later near Shechem, where he purchased land and built an altar. For the first time in the narrative, Jacob called God by a personal name: "God, the God of Israel." The God of Abraham and Isaac was finally becoming Jacob's own God.

TROUBLE AT SHECHEM

But Jacob was taking his time getting back to Bethel, the place where he had made his vow to God decades earlier. And the delay invited disaster.

While living near Shechem, Jacob's daughter Dinah was assaulted by the son of the local ruler. The young man then asked to marry her, and his father approached Jacob's family with a proposal for intermarriage between the two communities.

Jacob's sons, furious over their sister's violation, responded with deception. They agreed to the marriage on the condition that every man in the city be circumcised. The men of Shechem complied. Three days later, while the men were still recovering and unable to defend themselves, Simeon and Levi attacked the city and killed every male. The other brothers plundered the town.

Jacob was horrified. "You have brought trouble on me," he told Simeon and Levi. But his sons shot back, "Should he have treated our sister like a prostitute?"

There are no heroes in this chapter. Shechem's prince committed a terrible crime. Jacob was passive when he should have acted. And his sons responded with treachery and disproportionate violence that abused the covenant sign of circumcision as a weapon. The dysfunction that had been building in Jacob's family was now erupting into atrocity.

BACK TO BETHEL

God intervened. "Go up to Bethel and settle there," he told Jacob. It was time to stop stalling.

Before they left, Jacob ordered his household to get rid of every foreign god and idol in their possession. They handed over their false gods and even their earrings, which were associated with idol worship. Jacob buried them under a tree at Shechem. It was a decisive act of spiritual housecleaning, long overdue, and it signaled that Jacob was finally taking his role as spiritual leader of the family seriously.

God protected the family as they traveled. When they arrived at Bethel, Jacob built an altar and named it "God of the House of God." God appeared to him there and reaffirmed the covenant promises: a nation, kings, and land. The same promises he had made to Abraham and Isaac, now confirmed a final time to Israel.

But the journey from Bethel brought devastating loss. Rachel went into labor and died giving birth to her twelfth son. Her last words named the boy Ben-Oni, "son of my sorrow." Jacob renamed him Benjamin, "son of my right hand." Rachel, the woman Jacob had loved at first sight, the one he'd worked fourteen years to marry, was buried on the road near Bethlehem.

Then came another blow. Reuben, Jacob's firstborn, slept with Bilhah, Rachel's servant and Jacob's concubine. It was an act of rebellion, a challenge to Jacob's authority as head of the family. The text records it with devastating brevity: "And Israel heard of it." Jacob said nothing. But he remembered. Years later, on his deathbed, Reuben would lose the birthright because of this moment (49:3–4).

Isaac died at 180 years old, and Jacob and Esau buried their father together at Machpelah, just as Isaac and Ishmael had buried Abraham. The pattern held: divided brothers, reunited at a father's grave.

ESAU'S LINE

Genesis 36 closes the book on Esau. His genealogy is long and detailed, recording five generations of descendants who became chiefs, kings, and clans in the land of Edom. God's promise to Rebekah had been fulfilled: two nations had indeed come from her womb.

As with Ishmael before him, Genesis closes the non-chosen line before narrowing its focus to the chosen one. Esau's story is finished. Jacob's story continues. But Esau was not cursed or forgotten. He became a great nation, just as God said he would. And the brothers who had been enemies since the womb found enough peace to stand side by side at their father's funeral.

WHAT THIS MEANS FOR US

First, God sometimes has to break us before he can bless us. Jacob walked away from the Jabbok with a limp. He lost the ability to rely on his own strength. That wasn't a punishment. It was a gift. Sometimes God allows pain, failure, or weakness into our lives not to destroy us but to teach us to lean on him instead of ourselves. Paul learned the same lesson: "When I am weak, then I am strong" (2 Corinthians 12:10).

Second, reconciliation is possible even after deep betrayal. Jacob stole Esau's blessing. Esau swore to kill Jacob. Twenty years of silence followed. And yet, when they met again, Esau ran to embrace his brother. If that kind of forgiveness is possible between these two, it's possible in your family too. It may take time. It may take a long road. But God specializes in restoring what seems irreparably broken.

Third, delay in obeying God always costs more than obedience does. Jacob should have gone to Bethel immediately after returning to Canaan. Instead, he settled near Shechem, and the result was the worst crisis his family had faced. When God tells you to do something, do it. The longer you wait, the more complicated things get.

Fourth, your worst chapter isn't your last chapter. Jacob's family was a disaster. Rape, massacre, idolatry, adultery, death. And yet, out of this broken family, God built the twelve tribes of Israel and ultimately brought the Savior into the world. God doesn't need a perfect family. He needs a faithful God. And that's exactly what he is.

TALKING POINTS

1. **Jacob wrestled with God all night and walked away with a limp.** Why do you think God chose to permanently mark Jacob's body? What does Jacob's limp represent for his future?

2. **Esau ran to embrace the brother who had stolen his blessing.** What made that possible after twenty years? Have

you ever forgiven someone who wronged you deeply, or been forgiven by someone you wronged?

3. **Jacob ordered his family to give up their idols before going to Bethel.** What are some "idols" in our culture today, things that compete with God for first place in our hearts? Why is it important to deal with them before we can move forward spiritually?

4. **Rachel died giving birth to Benjamin. Jacob lost the love of his life.** How does grief show up in the rest of Jacob's story? How does knowing God is faithful help when life deals its hardest blows?

5. **Genesis always closes the story of the non-chosen line (Ishmael, Esau) before focusing on the chosen one.** What does it tell you about God that he keeps his promises even to the ones who aren't part of the main storyline?

The patriarchs are passing from the stage. Abraham is gone. Isaac is buried. Esau's story is closed. And Jacob, now called Israel, is an old man with a limp, a broken family, and twelve sons. One of those sons is about to disappear. And his story will change everything.

Turn the page.

13

FROM THE PIT TO THE PALACE

In Alexandre Dumas' *The Count of Monte Cristo*, a young sailor named Edmond Dantès has everything going for him. He's about to be promoted to captain. He's engaged to the woman he loves. His future is bright. Then, on the day that should have been the happiest of his life, three men who envy him hatch a plot. They write a false letter accusing him of treason. Edmond is arrested, tried without a fair hearing, and thrown into the Château d'If, a fortress prison on a tiny island off the coast of France. He is nineteen years old. He will spend the next fourteen years in a dark cell, forgotten by the world.

But in that prison, Edmond meets an old priest who teaches him languages, science, history, and philosophy. The priest also reveals the location of a hidden treasure. When Edmond finally escapes, he recovers the fortune and reinvents himself as the Count of Monte Cristo, one of the wealthiest and most powerful men in Europe. He uses that power to track down the men who destroyed his life and hold them accountable for what they did.

The story is about betrayal, suffering, patience, and the strange way that the worst thing that ever happened to someone can become the very thing that puts them in a position to save others.

That's the story of Joseph. Betrayed by his brothers. Sold into slavery. Falsely accused. Thrown into prison. Forgotten. And then, in a single day, lifted from a dungeon to the throne room of the most powerful nation on earth. But unlike Monte Cristo, Joseph didn't use his power for revenge. He used it to save the world.

THE DREAMER

Joseph was seventeen years old, the eleventh of Jacob's twelve sons and the firstborn of Rachel, Jacob's favorite wife. He was also, unmistakably, Jacob's favorite child. And Jacob made no effort to hide it.

He gave Joseph a special robe, an ornate garment that set him apart from his brothers. In the ancient world, a robe like this wasn't just clothing. It was a statement. It said: this son is different. This son doesn't do manual labor. This son is being groomed for leadership. Joseph's ten older brothers saw that robe every single day, and they hated him for it.

Things got worse when Joseph started having dreams. In the first dream, the brothers were binding sheaves of grain in a field, and their sheaves bowed down to Joseph's. In the second dream, the sun, moon, and eleven stars bowed down to Joseph. Even Jacob rebuked him for that one: "Will your mother and I and your brothers actually come and bow down to you?" But the text adds a telling detail: Jacob "kept the matter in mind." He was bothered by the dream, but he couldn't dismiss it either.

The brothers could dismiss it. They hated Joseph for the robe, and they hated him more for the dreams. What they didn't know was that these weren't just the fantasies of a spoiled teenager. God was giving Joseph a preview of the future. But between the dream and its fulfillment lay a road no one could have imagined.

THE PIT

Jacob sent Joseph to check on his brothers, who were tending flocks near Shechem. When the brothers saw him coming, still wearing that robe, they hatched a plan. "Here comes the dreamer," they sneered. "Let's kill him and throw him into a pit. Then we'll see what becomes of his dreams."

Reuben, the oldest, talked them out of murder, secretly planning to rescue Joseph later. But when Joseph arrived, they stripped off his robe, threw him into an empty cistern, and sat down to eat lunch. They ate while their brother screamed for help from the bottom of a hole. Years later, they would still remember the sound of his voice begging them to stop (42:21).

While they were eating, a caravan of traders passed by on the road to Egypt. Judah saw an opportunity. "What profit is it if we kill our brother?" he said. "Let's sell him instead." So they pulled Joseph out of the pit and sold him for twenty pieces of silver. Their own brother. The price of a slave.

Then they took his robe, dipped it in goat's blood, and brought it to Jacob. "We found this," they said. "Do you recognize it?" Jacob recognized it instantly. He tore his clothes, put on sackcloth, and mourned for weeks. "I will go down to the grave mourning my son," he said. His sons gathered around to comfort him, but he refused to be comforted.

The same sons who caused the grief stood there pretending to share it.

Meanwhile, Genesis 38 pauses the Joseph story to tell us what happened to Judah during those years. It's a difficult chapter—one of the most adult passages in Genesis—and it shows Judah at his worst: breaking a promise to his daughter-in-law Tamar, then condemning her for the very kind of sin he himself had committed. When Tamar exposed his hypocrisy, Judah was forced to confess, "She is more righteous than I." It was humiliating.

But that moment of exposure and confession appears to be the turning point in Judah's life. The man who callously sold his brother and deceived his father began, slowly, to become the man who would later offer his own life to save Benjamin. Without Genesis 38, the transformed Judah we meet at the climax of the Joseph story would make no sense. And from the son born to Tamar—a boy named Perez—would eventually come King David and, centuries later, Jesus himself. God was at work even in Judah's darkest chapter.

THE SLAVE

Joseph was taken to Egypt and sold to Potiphar, a high-ranking official in Pharaoh's court. And here the narrative makes a statement that will echo through the rest of Joseph's story: "The LORD was with Joseph."

That phrase appears four times in Genesis 39. It's the narrator's way of saying: watch what God does. Despite being a foreign slave in a pagan country, Joseph excelled at everything he touched. Potiphar noticed and promoted him to oversee his entire household. The text says Potiphar's house was blessed by God "because of Joseph." The promise God made to Abraham, that through his family all nations would be blessed, was already working itself out in a single Egyptian household.

Then disaster struck again. Potiphar's wife repeatedly tried to seduce Joseph. He refused every time. "How could I do such a wicked thing and sin against God?" he said. One day she grabbed his cloak, and Joseph fled the house, leaving the garment in her hands.

Once again, Joseph's clothing was used against him. His brothers had used his robe to convince Jacob he was dead. Now Potiphar's wife used his cloak to convince her husband that Joseph had attacked her. Potiphar threw Joseph into prison.

It was the second time Joseph had been stripped of his clothing and thrown into a hole because of someone else's sin. But the narrator repeats the refrain: "The LORD was with him."

THE PRISONER

In prison, Joseph again rose to a position of trust. The warden put him in charge of the other prisoners. And there, Joseph met two men who would change the course of history: Pharaoh's chief cupbearer and chief baker, both imprisoned for offending the king.

One night, each man had a dream. They were troubled because in Egypt, dreams were considered messages from the gods, and they had no access to professional interpreters. Joseph told them, "Interpretations belong to God. Tell me your dreams."

The cupbearer dreamed of a vine with three branches that budded, blossomed, and produced grapes. He squeezed the grapes into Pharaoh's cup and placed it in Pharaoh's hand. Joseph interpreted it: in three days, the cupbearer would be restored to his position.

The baker, encouraged by the good news, shared his dream. He was carrying three baskets of bread on his head, and birds were eating from the top basket. Joseph's interpretation was devastating: in three days, the baker would be executed.

Both interpretations came true exactly as Joseph said. The cupbearer went back to Pharaoh's court. The baker was killed. And Joseph asked the cupbearer for one small favor: "Remember me when things go well for you. Mention me to Pharaoh and get me out of this place."

The cupbearer forgot.

Joseph sat in prison for two more years.

THE THRONE ROOM

Then Pharaoh had a dream. He was standing by the Nile when seven fat, healthy cows came up from the water. Behind them came seven thin, ugly cows that devoured the fat ones. Then he dreamed again: seven plump heads of grain were swallowed by seven thin, scorched heads. Pharaoh woke up disturbed. He summoned every magician and wise man in Egypt. None of them could explain the dreams.

That's when the cupbearer finally remembered. "There was a young Hebrew in prison with me," he told Pharaoh. "He interpreted our dreams, and everything happened exactly as he said."

Joseph was rushed from the dungeon. He shaved, changed clothes, and stood before the most powerful man in the world. Pharaoh said, "I've heard you can interpret dreams." Joseph's answer was immediate and remarkable: "I cannot do it, but God will give Pharaoh the answer he needs."

In a culture where powerful men promoted themselves, where Pharaoh himself claimed to be a god, Joseph stood in the throne room and gave all the credit to someone else. That kind of humility could have gotten him sent right back to prison. Instead, it changed the world.

Joseph explained the dreams. Seven years of extraordinary abundance were coming to Egypt, followed by seven years of devastating famine. The famine would be so severe that the years of plenty would be completely forgotten. The dreams came in pairs because the matter was firmly decided by God and would happen soon.

Then Joseph did something audacious. Without being asked, he proposed a plan. Appoint a wise administrator to oversee the collection of grain during the seven good years. Store twenty percent of each harvest. Build up reserves so massive that when the famine hit, Egypt would survive.

Pharaoh looked at this thirty-year-old former prisoner and said, "Can we find anyone like this man, one in whom is the spirit of God?" He took off his signet ring and placed it on Joseph's finger. He dressed him in fine linen, hung a gold chain around his neck, and made him ride in the second chariot. Joseph, the boy from the pit, the slave, the prisoner, was now the second most powerful person in Egypt.

He was given an Egyptian name and an Egyptian wife. He oversaw the collection of grain during seven years of abundance so extraordinary that they eventually stopped keeping records because the amount was beyond measuring. He had two sons: Manasseh, meaning "God has made me forget all my hardship," and Ephraim, meaning "God has made me fruitful in the land of my suffering."

Those names tell you everything about where Joseph's heart was. He wasn't bitter. He wasn't scheming for revenge. He was grateful. He could see, even if he couldn't explain it all yet, that God had been with him in the pit, in the prison, and now in the palace. Every terrible chapter of his life had been leading somewhere.

Then the famine came. And it spread beyond Egypt to every surrounding nation. The whole world came to Egypt to buy grain. And the man standing between the world and starvation was a Hebrew slave who had been sold by his own brothers for twenty pieces of silver.

WHAT THIS MEANS FOR US

First, God is present in your worst moments. "The LORD was with Joseph" is repeated in the slave quarters and the prison cell, not just the palace. God didn't show up when Joseph's circumstances improved. He was there the whole time. If you're going through something terrible right now, that truth hasn't changed. God's presence doesn't depend on your comfort.

Second, other people's sins cannot derail God's plan for your life. Joseph's brothers sold him. Potiphar's wife lied about him. The cupbearer forgot him. At every turn, someone else's sin knocked Joseph down. But none of it could knock him off the path God had laid out. People can hurt you. They can delay you. But they cannot cancel what God has determined to do through you.

Third, faithfulness in small things prepares you for big things. Joseph managed Potiphar's house well. He managed the prison well. And when the moment came to manage a nation, he was ready. The years of invisible faithfulness weren't wasted. They were training. How you handle what nobody sees determines what God entrusts to you when everyone is watching.

Fourth, God's timing is not your timing. Thirteen years passed between Joseph's dreams and his rise to power. Thirteen years of slavery, false accusation, and imprisonment. If you had asked Joseph at year six whether God's promises were real, he might have struggled to answer. But God was working the entire time. The wait is not the absence of God's plan. It's part of it.

TALKING POINTS

1. **Joseph's brothers hated him partly because of Jacob's favoritism.** How does favoritism damage a family? What can parents and siblings do to avoid it?

2. **Joseph refused Potiphar's wife by saying, "How could I sin against God?" He didn't say "against Potiphar" or "against your marriage."** Why do you think he framed it that way? How does seeing sin as an offense against God change the way you think about temptation?

3. **The cupbearer forgot Joseph for two years.** Have you ever felt forgotten by someone who promised to help? How do you keep trusting God when people let you down?

4. **Joseph told Pharaoh, "I cannot do it, but God will give you the answer."** What made that such a risky thing to say? Why is it important to give God credit even when it might not help your situation?

5. Joseph named his sons "God made me forget my hardship" and "God made me fruitful in suffering." What does it look like to find gratitude in the middle of pain? Is it possible to be thankful for what God is doing even before the suffering ends?

The famine is spreading. The world is desperate. And somewhere in Canaan, an old man named Jacob is running out of food. He doesn't know that the brother his sons sold into slavery is the one person on earth who can save them.

But God knows. And he's been planning this reunion for twenty-two years.

Turn the page.

14

THE REVEAL

In Pixar's *Coco*, a boy named Miguel dreams of becoming a musician. But his family has banned music for generations because Miguel's great-great-grandfather, a musician, once abandoned his wife and daughter to chase fame. The family remembers him with bitterness. His photo has been torn from the family shrine. His name is never spoken.

When Miguel accidentally crosses into the Land of the Dead, he meets a ragged skeleton named Héctor who is slowly being forgotten. Héctor is desperate: if no one in the living world remembers him, he will vanish forever. He begs Miguel to take his photo back and place it on the family altar so that someone, anyone, will remember him.

It turns out that Héctor *is* Miguel's great-great-grandfather. He never abandoned his family. He was murdered by his best friend, Ernesto de la Cruz, who stole his songs, took credit for his music, and erased him from history. The man the family hated was actually the man who had loved them most. He had been trying to come home the night he was killed.

The climax of the movie is the moment of revelation. The truth comes out. The villain is exposed. And Miguel races back to the living world to sing to his great-grandmother before Héctor disappears forever. "Remember me," he sings, and the old woman's eyes light up. She remembers. The family is restored. The forgotten one is brought home.

Genesis 42–45 is the Bible's greatest reveal. For twenty-two years, Joseph's family believed he was dead. His brothers knew the truth but buried it under layers of guilt and silence. Then, in the throne room of Egypt, the most powerful man in the nation looked at his ten brothers and said three words that changed everything: "I am Joseph."

THE BROTHERS COME TO EGYPT

The famine that Joseph had predicted spread across the entire ancient world, and Canaan was hit hard. Jacob's family was running out of food. When Jacob heard that grain was available in Egypt, he sent ten of his sons to buy some. He kept Benjamin, his youngest, at home. After losing Joseph, Jacob couldn't bear the thought of risking Rachel's only other son.

The ten brothers arrived in Egypt and were brought before the governor in charge of grain distribution. They bowed face-down before him. They had no idea they were bowing to Joseph.

But Joseph recognized them instantly. And in that moment, he remembered the dreams from his youth: sheaves of grain bowing to his sheaf, the sun and moon and stars bowing to him. The dreams were coming true, right before his eyes.

Joseph didn't reveal himself. Instead, he spoke harshly. He accused them of being spies, sent to scout Egypt's defenses during the famine. The brothers protested: "We are all sons of one man. We are honest men." They mentioned their family: twelve brothers total, one who "is no more" and the youngest who remained with their father in Canaan.

Joseph threw them in prison for three days. Then he released all of them except Simeon, who was kept as a hostage. The rest could go home, but they had to bring Benjamin back on their next trip. That was the condition.

As they discussed the situation among themselves, not knowing Joseph could understand every word, the guilt came flooding out. "We are being punished because of our brother," they said. "We saw how distressed he was when he pleaded with us for his life, but we would not listen." Reuben added, "Didn't I tell you not to sin against the boy? Now we must give an accounting for his blood."

Joseph turned away and wept. Twenty-two years, and the wound was still fresh.

He filled their sacks with grain and secretly returned their money. When they discovered the silver on the road home, they were terrified. "What is this that God has done to us?" they asked. They could feel the walls closing in.

THE RETURN WITH BENJAMIN

Back in Canaan, Jacob refused to let Benjamin go. "Joseph is no more and Simeon is no more," he said. "Now you want to take Benjamin? Everything is against me!" Reuben offered his own two sons as a guarantee, but Jacob wouldn't budge.

Then the food ran out.

It was Judah who finally broke through. He offered himself

as the guarantee for Benjamin's safety: "If I do not bring him back to you, then let me bear the blame forever." This was a different Judah than the one who had proposed selling Joseph into slavery twenty-two years earlier. Something had changed in him. He was no longer looking out for himself. He was willing to stake his own life on his brother's return.

Jacob relented. He sent the brothers back with double the money, gifts of honey, spices, and nuts, and Benjamin.

When Joseph saw Benjamin, his full brother, the only other son of his mother Rachel, he had to leave the room. He went into a private chamber and sobbed. Then he washed his face, composed himself, and came back out.

Joseph hosted a feast. He seated the brothers in birth order, which astonished them. How could this Egyptian official know their ages? He sent food from his own table, but Benjamin's portion was five times larger than anyone else's. Joseph was watching. Would the brothers resent Benjamin the way they had resented him? Would the old jealousy surface?

It didn't. They ate and drank together, and for one evening, the family was almost whole.

THE FINAL TEST

The next morning, Joseph sent the brothers on their way. But he had ordered his steward to hide his personal silver cup in Benjamin's sack. Before the brothers had gotten far, Joseph's men overtook them and accused them of theft.

The brothers were horrified. They were so confident of their innocence that they made a rash vow: "If any of your servants is found to have it, he will die, and the rest of us will become slaves." The steward searched the sacks, starting with the oldest and working down. When he opened Benjamin's sack, the cup was there.

They tore their clothes in grief and returned to the city.

This was the real test. Joseph had engineered the exact scenario his brothers had faced twenty-two years earlier. The favored son of Rachel was in trouble. They could walk away and leave Benjamin to his fate, just as they had left Joseph in the pit. They could go home, tell Jacob that Benjamin was gone, and move on with their lives. Nobody would stop them.

They all went back.

JUDAH'S SPEECH

Standing before Joseph, Judah delivered one of the most powerful speeches in all of Scripture. He didn't make excuses. He didn't try to shift blame. He told the whole story: their father's grief over Joseph, the agony of sending Benjamin, the old man's fragile heart that couldn't survive losing another son.

"God has uncovered your servants' guilt," he said. It was more than a statement about the cup. It may have been a confession about everything: the pit, the blood-stained robe, the twenty-two years of lies.

Then Judah made his offer: "Please let your servant remain here as my lord's slave in place of the boy, and let the boy return with his brothers. How can I go back to my father if the boy is not with me? Don't make me watch the misery that would come on my father."

Judah, the brother who had sold Joseph for profit, was now offering to become a slave so that Benjamin could go free. The man who had watched his father's heart shatter without a word was now willing to spend the rest of his life in an Egyptian dungeon rather than see his father grieve again.

The brothers had changed. The test was over.

I AM JOSEPH

Joseph couldn't hold it together any longer. He ordered every Egyptian out of the room. And then he wept so loudly that the sound carried through the walls and was heard throughout Pharaoh's palace.

"I am Joseph!" he said. "Is my father still alive?"

His brothers couldn't answer. They were terrified. The word used for their reaction describes the kind of paralyzing fear a soldier feels when he realizes a battle is lost. They were standing before the second most powerful man in Egypt, and he was the brother they had thrown into a pit and sold into slavery. They expected to die.

But Joseph said something no one expected. "Come close to me," he said. They stepped forward. "I am your brother Joseph, the one you sold into Egypt. And now, do not be distressed and do not be angry with yourselves for selling me here, because it was to save lives that God sent me ahead of you."

Three times in his speech, Joseph said "God sent me." Not "you sent me." God. Joseph didn't minimize what his brothers had done. He didn't pretend it hadn't been evil. But in twenty-two years of suffering, he had come to see something that changed everything: God had been behind the whole story. The pit, the slavery, the prison, the cupbearer's forgetfulness, the dreams of Pharaoh, all of it was God positioning Joseph to save the world from famine and to preserve his own family alive.

"It was not you who sent me here, but God."

That sentence is one of the most theologically important in the entire Old Testament. It doesn't excuse sin. It doesn't erase pain. But it reveals something breathtaking about how God works. He takes the worst things human beings do to each other and weaves them into a plan that accomplishes good beyond anything anyone imagined. Joseph's brothers meant it for evil. God meant it for good.

Joseph told his brothers to hurry home and bring their father and the entire family to Egypt. Pharaoh, delighted at the news, offered them the best land in the country. Joseph loaded them with provisions, gave each brother new clothes, and gave Benjamin five sets of garments and three hundred pieces of silver. Clothing had started this whole disaster. Now clothing was part of the healing.

As they left, Joseph gave one last instruction: "Don't quarrel on the way." The word is better translated "don't be afraid." He knew their guilt would eat at them on the long road home. He was telling them to let it go.

When the brothers reached Canaan and told Jacob that Joseph was alive and ruling all of Egypt, Jacob's heart went numb. He didn't believe them. But when he saw the carts Joseph had sent and heard every detail of what had happened, something inside the old man came back to life. "I'm convinced!" he said. "My son Joseph is still alive. I will go and see him before I die."

The father who had been mourning for twenty-two years was about to hold his son again.

WHAT THIS MEANS FOR US

First, real repentance produces real change. Judah's transformation is the quiet miracle of the Joseph story. The man who sold his brother for profit offered to become a slave for his brother's freedom. That kind of change doesn't happen overnight. It takes years of conviction, failure, and slow growth. But it's real, and God honors it.

Second, forgiveness doesn't mean forgetting. Joseph wept every time he was alone with his memories. The pain was still real after twenty-two years. But he chose not to use his power for revenge. Forgiveness isn't pretending something didn't happen. It's choosing not to let what happened control what happens next.

Third, God's plan is bigger than your pain. Joseph spent thirteen years in slavery and prison before he saw even a glimpse of what God was doing. He couldn't have known, sitting in that dungeon, that he was being positioned to save millions of lives. When you can't see the plan, trust the Planner. He is working in your story, even in the chapters that make no sense yet.

Fourth, the test reveals the heart. Joseph tested his brothers not to punish them but to find out who they had become. God does the same with us. Difficult circumstances aren't always punishment. Sometimes they're the test that shows—to God and to ourselves—what we're really made of.

TALKING POINTS

1. **Joseph tested his brothers to see if they had changed.** Why do you think he didn't just reveal himself right away? What was he looking for?

2. **Judah offered to take Benjamin's place as a slave.** How is that different from the Judah we met in Genesis 37? What do you think caused the change?

3. **Joseph said, "It was not you who sent me here, but God."** How can both things be true—that the brothers sinned *and* that God was behind the story? Does God's involvement excuse the brothers' behavior?

4. **Joseph forgave his brothers even though the pain was still fresh after twenty-two years.** What does that tell you about forgiveness? Is it a feeling or a decision?

5. **Jacob's "heart went numb" when he heard Joseph was alive. He couldn't believe it. Then he saw the evidence and his spirit revived.** What helps you believe promises that seem too good to be true?

The family is coming back together. Jacob will see his son again. And the entire clan of Israel is about to move to Egypt, where God will grow them from a family into a nation.

But before the story ends, an old man has one more thing to do. He has blessings to give, a future to foretell, and a God to praise for keeping every promise he ever made.

Turn the page.

15

YOU MEANT IT FOR EVIL

In Charles Dickens' *A Tale of Two Cities*, a man named Sydney Carton has wasted his life. He's brilliant but aimless, a London lawyer who drinks too much and cares too little. He loves a woman named Lucie Manette, but she marries someone else, a good man named Charles Darnay. Carton watches from the edges, convinced his own story is going nowhere.

Then the French Revolution erupts. Darnay is arrested in Paris and sentenced to the guillotine. Lucie and her daughter will lose a husband and father. And Carton, the man who has never done anything that mattered, makes the decision that defines his entire life. He sneaks into Darnay's cell, swaps places with him, and goes to the guillotine instead. His final words, imagined by the narrator, are among the most famous in all of literature: "It is a far, far better thing that I do, than I have ever done; it is a far, far better rest that I go to than I have ever known."

Carton's death isn't a tragedy. It's a redemption. A life that looked wasted turns out to have been leading somewhere all along. And because of his sacrifice, a family survives. The people he loved get a future he chose to give them.

Genesis 46–50 is a story about lives that looked wasted — broken by deception, scarred by betrayal, spent in exile — that turn out to have been leading somewhere all along. A father who spent his life scheming dies full of faith. A son who suffered for twenty-two years speaks the sentence that makes sense of the entire book: "You meant it for evil, but God meant it for good." And a coffin sits in Egypt, not as a dead end but as a promise. The story isn't over. The best is still to come.

COMING HOME TO EGYPT

When Jacob heard that Joseph was alive, his spirit revived. But before he left Canaan, he stopped at Beersheba, the southern border of the Promised Land, and offered sacrifices to God. It was as if he needed to ask permission before crossing the line.

God spoke to him in a vision: "Do not be afraid to go down to Egypt, for I will make you into a great nation there. I will go down to Egypt with you, and I will surely bring you back again. And Joseph's own hand will close your eyes."

Those words mattered. God had forbidden Isaac from going to Egypt during a famine (26:2). Jacob needed to know this move was different. And God gave him three promises: a nation would grow from his family in Egypt, God himself would go with them, and Jacob would not die without seeing Joseph again.

Seventy members of Jacob's family made the journey. It was a small number, barely enough to fill a school bus. But that number would explode over the next four centuries into a nation of millions. The seventy who entered Egypt were a seed. God would do the growing.

When the caravan arrived, Joseph rode out in his chariot to meet his father. The moment they saw each other, Joseph threw his arms around Jacob's neck and wept for a long time. Jacob said, "Now I am ready to die, since I have seen for myself that you are still alive."

It was the reunion of a father who had mourned for twenty-two years and a son who had suffered for just as long. Neither had given up hope, though both had every reason to.

Pharaoh gave Jacob's family the land of Goshen, a fertile region in the northeast corner of the Nile delta, perfect for shepherds and flocks. When Jacob was brought before Pharaoh, the old patriarch blessed the most powerful ruler on earth. Then Pharaoh asked him a simple question: "How old are you?"

Jacob's answer is one of the most revealing lines in Genesis: "The years of my pilgrimage are a hundred and thirty. My years have been few and difficult, and they do not equal the years of the pilgrimage of my fathers."

Few and difficult. That was Jacob's summary of his own life. He had been a deceiver, an exile, a victim of Laban's treachery, a father who lost his favorite son, and a man who had wrestled with God and walked away limping. He didn't sugarcoat it. But the fact that he called his life a "pilgrimage" tells you everything about where his faith had landed. He was a traveler. This world was not his home. He was looking for something better.

THE BLESSINGS

As Jacob neared the end of his life, he did what Abraham and Isaac had done before him. He blessed the next generation.

First, he adopted Joseph's two sons, Ephraim and Manasseh,

as his own, effectively giving Joseph a double share of the inheritance. When Joseph presented the boys for the blessing, he positioned Manasseh, the firstborn, at Jacob's right hand and Ephraim, the younger, at his left. But Jacob deliberately crossed his hands, placing his right hand on Ephraim's head. Joseph tried to correct him. Jacob refused. "I know, my son, I know," he said. The younger would be greater than the older. The same reversal that had defined Jacob's own life was now being passed forward. God's choices don't follow the world's rules.

Then Jacob gathered all twelve of his sons and spoke prophetically over each one. Some blessings were glowing. Others were devastating. Reuben lost the birthright because of his sin with Bilhah. Simeon and Levi were rebuked for the massacre at Shechem. But Judah received the most significant prophecy of all: "The scepter will not depart from Judah, nor the ruler's staff from between his feet, until he to whom it belongs shall come, and the obedience of the nations shall be his."

That prophecy pointed far beyond anything Judah's tribe would accomplish in the Old Testament. It pointed to a king from Judah's line who would rule the nations. It pointed to Jesus.

Joseph received a blessing overflowing with abundance and protection, a father's love poured out in prophetic language that acknowledged everything Joseph had endured and everything God had done through him.

When the blessings were finished, Jacob gave his final instruction: "Bury me with my fathers in the cave of Machpelah, in the land of Canaan." Even in death, Jacob was declaring his faith in the promise. Canaan was home. Egypt was a stop along the way.

Then Jacob drew his feet up into the bed and breathed his last.

A FUNERAL FOR A PATRIARCH

Joseph wept over his father and ordered the physicians to embalm him in the Egyptian custom. Egypt mourned Jacob for seventy days, nearly as long as they would mourn a pharaoh. Then Joseph led a massive funeral procession back to Canaan, accompanied by Egyptian officials, chariots, and horsemen. It was a state funeral for a Hebrew shepherd, a testimony to how deeply God had blessed Jacob's family through Joseph's position in Egypt.

They buried Jacob in the cave at Machpelah, beside Abraham and Sarah, beside Isaac and Rebekah, beside Leah. The cave that Abraham had purchased at an outrageous price was now the resting place of three generations of the covenant family. A cemetery had become the most important piece of real estate in the history of the world, a quiet declaration that God's promises outlast death.

YOU MEANT IT FOR EVIL

After the funeral, the brothers panicked. With Jacob gone, they feared Joseph would finally take his revenge. They sent a message claiming that Jacob had asked Joseph to forgive them, though whether Jacob had actually said this is unclear. Then they came and fell before him, offering to be his slaves.

Joseph wept when he heard their message. Even after everything, even after the reconciliation in Egypt, his brothers still couldn't believe they were truly forgiven. Guilt had followed them for more than two decades, and they were still waiting for the other shoe to drop.

Joseph's response is the theological summit of the entire book of Genesis. "Don't be afraid," he said. "Am I in the place of God? You intended to harm me, but God intended it for good to accomplish what is now being done, the saving of many lives."

That sentence holds together two truths that seem impossible to reconcile. First, the brothers sinned. What they did was evil. Joseph didn't minimize it or wave it away. Second, God was behind it. Not causing the evil, but working through it, weaving it into a plan so vast that the brothers couldn't have imagined it when they threw Joseph into the pit. The same act that was wicked from a human perspective was, from God's perspective, the means by which an entire region of the world would be saved from starvation and the covenant family would be preserved.

This doesn't make sin okay. It doesn't remove consequences. But it reveals something breathtaking about the God of Genesis: he is so powerful and so good that he can take the worst things human beings do and fold them into a plan that accomplishes more good than the evil ever destroyed.

Joseph promised to provide for his brothers and their children. He reassured them. He spoke kindly to them. The man who had every right to exact revenge chose mercy instead.

A COFFIN IN EGYPT

Joseph lived to be 110 years old, long enough to see his great-great-grandchildren. As his death approached, he gathered his brothers and spoke his final words: "I am about to die. But God will surely come to your aid and take you up out of this land to the land he promised on oath to Abraham, Isaac, and Jacob."

Then he made them swear an oath: "When God comes to your aid, you must carry my bones up from this place."

Joseph died and was embalmed. But he was not buried in Canaan. His body was placed in a coffin in Egypt. And there Genesis ends: with a coffin, a promise, and an expectation.

That coffin is the final image of the book, and it's deliberate. It says: this story is not over. The promise of land has not been fulfilled. The family is in the wrong country. Everything is in place for the next chapter, but the next chapter hasn't happened yet.

For four hundred years, that coffin sat in Egypt. Generation after generation of Israelites grew up knowing it was there, knowing what it represented: God will come. God will bring us home. Don't forget the promise.

And when Moses finally led Israel out of Egypt, he took Joseph's bones with him (Exodus 13:19). The promise was kept. The coffin came home.

WHAT THIS MEANS FOR US

First, God can bring good out of the worst evil. Genesis 50:20 is the verse that makes sense of the entire book. From the fall in the garden to the pit at Dothan, every act of human evil has been met by a God who refuses to let sin have the last word. That doesn't mean sin doesn't matter. It means God is bigger.

Second, forgiveness is the end of the story, not bitterness. Joseph had every reason to be bitter. He chose grace instead.

He didn't wait for his brothers to earn forgiveness. He gave it freely because he could see God's hand in his suffering. If you are holding onto anger toward someone who wronged you, Joseph's story says: let it go. Not because what they did was okay, but because God is writing a bigger story than your pain.

Third, dying in faith is the best gift you can give your family. Jacob and Joseph both died with God's promises on their lips. They didn't leave their families with money or power. They left them with faith. The most important thing you can pass on to the people you love isn't your stuff. It's your trust in God.

Fourth, the story isn't over. Genesis ends with a coffin in Egypt, not a triumphal entry into Canaan. The promises haven't all been fulfilled yet. But that's not a failure. It's an invitation. God is still writing. The exodus is coming. The law is coming. The prophets are coming. The King is coming. And one day, everything that was promised to Abraham, Isaac, and Jacob will be fulfilled in ways they never imagined, through a carpenter's son from the tribe of Judah who will reign forever.

TALKING POINTS

1. **Jacob described his life as "few and difficult." Yet he died full of faith.** How can someone go through a hard life and still trust God at the end? What makes the difference?

2. **Joseph said, "You meant it for evil, but God meant it for good."** How does knowing that God works through even evil circumstances change the way you think about hard things that have happened to you?

3. **Joseph forgave his brothers even though their guilt still haunted them decades later.** Why is it so hard for people

to accept forgiveness, even when it's freely offered? Have you ever struggled to believe you were truly forgiven?

4. **Genesis ends with a coffin in Egypt and an unfulfilled promise.** Why do you think God left the story unfinished? What does that teach us about living between promise and fulfillment?

5. **The entire book of Genesis moves from creation to a coffin.** But Joseph's last words are full of hope: "God will surely come to your aid." How does the hope of something better in the future help you endure the difficulties of today?

And so the book of beginnings ends—not with a triumph but with a promise.

Go back to the first page and remember where we started. A universe spoken into existence. A garden where God walked with the people he made. A world so good that the Creator looked at it and smiled. Then a serpent, a piece of fruit, and a choice that broke everything. A murder. A flood. A tower. A scattering. By the end of chapter 11, the human race was fractured, scattered, and far from God.

But God wasn't done. He called one man out of a pagan city and made him a promise so enormous it would take the rest of the Bible to fulfill. Through Abraham, Isaac, Jacob, and Joseph—through their faith and their failures, their obedience and their stubbornness, their mountaintop encounters with God and their face-down-in-the-dirt mistakes—God carried that promise forward. He never dropped it. Not once.

And now, at the end of Genesis, the promise is alive but not yet fulfilled. The family has become a clan of seventy. They're in the wrong country. The land of Canaan is still occupied by other nations. The blessing to all peoples is still a distant hope. And a coffin sits in Egypt, holding the bones of a man who made his family swear: God will come for you. Carry me home when he does.

That coffin will sit there for four hundred years. Four centuries of silence, then slavery, then suffering. It will look like God has forgotten everything. It will feel like the promises were just stories old people told their children at night.

But the promises were never just stories. And God never forgets.

One day, a baby will be hidden in a basket on the Nile. A bush will catch fire and not burn up. A shepherd will stand before a king and say, "Let my people go." Plagues will fall. A sea will part. A mountain will shake. And when Israel finally marches out of Egypt, someone will remember to grab a coffin.

The story of Genesis doesn't end in Genesis. It ends in a stable in Bethlehem, where the seed of Abraham, the lion of Judah, the son of David was born to a virgin and laid in a manger. It ends on a cross outside Jerusalem, where the God who provided a ram on Moriah provided something greater—his own Son, the Lamb who takes away the sin of the world. It ends at an empty tomb, where the curse of death that entered the world in a garden was broken forever.

And it ends with a promise that still hasn't been fully kept. Jesus told his followers, "I will come again." We're still waiting. We're still living between the promise and the fulfillment, just like Abraham, just like Joseph, just like that coffin in Egypt.

But if Genesis teaches us anything, it's this: God keeps his promises. Every single one. He kept them through barrenness and famine, through deception and betrayal, through four hundred years of slavery and a cross that looked like the end of everything. He will keep the ones he's made to you.

So hold on. Keep trusting. The story isn't over.

It's only the beginning.

www.ingramcontent.com/pod-product-compliance
Lightning Source LLC
Chambersburg PA
CBHW050942050726
47592CB00007B/2399